HEART-CENTERED LEADERSHIP

UNIQUE PATHWAYS, APPROACHES AND STRATEGIES
TO SOUL-ALIGNED SUCCESS

KATELYN ANNEMARIE BRUSH   ALLISON BRATSCH
ALYCIA CAMACHO   ALYSEMARIE GALLAGHER WARREN
BRIENNA BECKER   CARLA MARCONI   CLARISSA TU
ELIZABETH MARTIN   HANNAH IRENE DUFFY
HELEN LIM   HELEN STAGG   JOE DINARDO
JOHN PAUL KINGSTON   KATIE FORSE
LAUREN MEGAN VALDES   MARA ELAINE WILLEMIN
MATTHEW ALLYN MICHALEK   MICHELLE BADAGLIACCA
MOLLY ROSE RASANEN   SOPHIE SHEPHERD
TARA THERESE BULIN   TAYLOR SLEAFORD
WHITNEY KEAR

EXALTED PUBLISHING HOUSE

Copyright © 2022 by Katelyn Annemarie Brush

All rights reserved. Apart from any fair dealing for the purposes of research or private study, or criticism or review, as permitted under the Copyright, Designs, and Patents Act 1988, this publication may only be reproduced, stored, or transmitted, in any form or by any means, with the prior permission in writing of the copyright owner, or in the case of the reprographic reproduction in accordance with the terms of licensees issued by the Copyright Licensing Agency. Enquires concerning reproduction outside those terms should be sent to the publisher.

The publisher takes no legal responsibility for the details inside the stories of this book. The words and opinions are the writer's own, the memories they describe are their lived experience and the publisher does not have any evidence that those stories are untrue. The publisher has chosen to trust the authors and has not done them the disservice of fact-checking every version of events. Memoirs are stories from one person's vantage point.

Although the publisher and the authors have made every effort to ensure that the information in this book was correct at press time and while this publication is designed to provide accurate information in regard to the subject matter covered, the publisher and the authors assume no responsibility for errors, inaccuracies, omissions, or any other consistencies herein and hereby disclaim any liability to any party for any loss, damage, or disruption caused by errors or omissions, whether such errors or omissions results from negligence, accident, or any other cause.

Medical Disclaimer: The ideas, concepts and opinions expressed in this book are intended to be used for educational purposes only. The book is offered with the understanding that the author or publisher is not rendering medical advice of any kind, nor is the book intended to replace medical advice, to diagnose, prescribe or treat any disease, condition, illness or injury.

CONTENTS

Introduction	v
1. It's All About The Journey	1
AlyseMarie Gallagher Warren	9
2. Leading with Love	10
Helen Stagg	19
3. My Journey to Becoming a Securely-Attached Leader	20
Allison Bratsch	29
4. Heart-Centered, Feelings Focused	30
Joe Dinardo	39
5. Unstoppable	40
Sophie Shepherd	49
6. The Gateway to Self-Empowerment	50
Carla Marconi	59
7. Empower the Ember & Honor the Human	60
Hannah Irene Duffy	69
8. Turning Ashes to Gold—A Path to Liberation & Leadership Through the Body	70
Lauren Megan Valdes	81
9. Your Inner Nature Leads The Way	82
Alycia Camacho	93
10. Heart Medicine	94
Helen Lim	103
11. Living Vibrantly	104
Brienna Becker	115
12. How my Heart was Influenced by Nature and Sports	116
John Paul Kingston	125
13. Revolutionizing Heart Centered Healthcare	126
Elizabeth Martin	137
14. Hearing the Whispers of the Heart	138
Katie Forse	147
15. Simultaneous Healing: Together We Walk—As We Learn, Become Aware, and Evolve	148
Tara Therese Bulin, Ph.D, LCSW-R	157
16. Why You Need A Quarter Life Crisis	158

	Matthew Allyn Michalek	169
17.	The Unpaved Path	170
	Molly Rose Rasanen	179
18.	Redesigning Leadership	180
	Taylor Sleaford	189
19.	Following the Intuitive Breadcrumbs	190
	Michelle Badagliacca	199
20.	Becoming At One	200
	Clarissa Tu	211
21.	Your Impact Is In Your Character	212
	Whitney Kear	223
22.	The New American Dream: Sharing the Heart of the Matter	225
	Mara Elaine Willemin	235
23.	About Exalted Publishing House	236
	About Katelyn Annemarie Brush	239

INTRODUCTION

* * *

Leaders. They are quoted on mural walls in cities and towns worldwide. Their writings are read centuries after they've left this earth. Their acts of service have permeated the pages of every history book and have shaped our world in more ways than we can count. They are individuals who set the stage for what's possible when we live bravely and trust in our power. And while this can be said for many leaders, the difference between a leader and a heart-centered leader is unmistakable.

Heart-centered leadership is aligned with the greatest good for all.

It focuses on humanity as a whole over ego, power, and profit.

It's an active practice that a person chooses–first within themselves and then in the world around them.

This book was written with the intention to show the human side of being a leader, to peel back the curtain, and let it be known that everyone has the ability to lead in this way.

INTRODUCTION

I know you picked up this book because it's clear to you that the significance of leadership is massive. The world evolves forward or regresses in accordance with the quality of leadership.

When most people think of leadership, they think of the person who owns a business, is in a managerial role or holds political power. This book serves as an invitation for us all to step up as heart-centered leaders regardless of our positions or current circumstances.

When I think of leadership, I see a wide spectrum of relationships. The first manager I had who micromanaged teenagers with her hot temper as we scooped ice cream. The woman who generously offered her time to me when I was starting my business while knowing we could be seen as competitors but chose to see us as teammates with a like-minded cause. I think of my parents and grandparents and how they guided me. Then I also think of the shift manager who was twice my age and sexually harassed me. I think of the boss who stood up for me in a crowded room of customers. Memories flood in of a previous employer who's friends and employees spoke highly of him, and I remember how his character was the reason employees encouraged half their family to work at the man's company. Memories of a boss who's clients complained about her strict nature. There is no singular way to lead, but when I think of the leaders who inspire me, it's the ones who thought beyond themselves, who opened their hearts to the world and consciously created a legacy that would leave a positive impact for their family, their employee's families, and the world around them.

I'm sure you have stories that span the wide spectrum of leadership styles, too. Observing the duality of a topic is often how we find ourselves becoming clear on our own values.

The point is, we're all here because we believe that putting this book into the world could change billions of lives and show others it's possible to achieve incredible things with compassion. As a collective, we are rewriting the narrative and setting a higher standard for the leaders of tomorrow.

INTRODUCTION

Heart-centered leadership goes beyond the title that a person holds. It addresses a person's character, their integrity, what they stand for, and how they stand. Inside the pages of this book, you will read the stories of 22 diverse and dynamic leaders from all over the world who embody these new qualities of leadership.

When we think about making a positive impact, most people think about the leaders who generated massive changes like Ghandi, Martin Luther King, Mother Teresa and the like. They think of these really big moments. A speech that went down in history, a protest that changed the world; and while these things have inspired us and were incredibly pivotal to human history, positive change doesn't always have to be that way.

Change doesn't always need to make it into the history books in order to be valuable. It can also happen in simple, day-to-day ways. A million small moments happened before the landmark events of these great leaders. Before they stood in front of the world, speaking out against injustice, they stood in front of the mirror, when no one was watching, and bravely held themselves to a higher standard.

The stories from our history books are the reminder that everything compounds and builds up, strengthening our muscles and developing the endurance necessary for us to make the ripple effect our legacy is capable of. We want you to remember that the mundane tasks, the day-to-day, and challenging initiation portals of life all add up. We want you to keep going, stay inspired, and see yourself as someone who can change the world.

The stories within this book are from human beings not much different from you. They've struggled with imposter syndrome, faced health challenges, married, divorced, had their hearts broken, changed jobs, changed business models, lost loved ones, and set boundaries with loved ones. One person could have written this book, but instead we asked 22 authors to help write this book. Why? Because it's not about one person. There is no one, linear path. It's complex and beautiful all at once. Heart-centered leadership isn't for one 'special' or

INTRODUCTION

'famous' or 'perfect' person… it's for all of us and at this point in time, it requires all of us.

Our vision for this book was to **inspire the masses.**

After years of entrepreneurship, helping start ups and getting behind the scenes with hundreds of founders, CEOs and company teams, I felt the pull to bring it all together within a book on leadership. The idea existed for a few years, but to be honest, it never felt fully right.

I put the idea off again and again, until one day, in a conversation with my friend, Bridget Sicsko, the founder of Exalted Publishing House, this book communicated how it wanted to be written. Not by one leader, but by many. We are so proud to have brought these authors together from all over the world, people with all different backgrounds, experiences and expertise. This multi-author book is a representation of heart-centered leadership because it's about all of us.

When we tell our stories and we share our perspectives, a new world is created. Sometimes we speak that world into existence, sometimes we write it. What's certain is that our futures and our potential are not up to chance, they're up to us.

IT'S ALL ABOUT THE JOURNEY

Let's drop in for the journey we are about to embark on. My guides are already here with me and, as you read, they are with you too. You are not alone. You are safe. You are here, in this now. You are fully supported. However you feel at this moment is absolutely valid. Sink into this space and feeling; let your guard down. Come into my bubble of authentic truth and be completely who you are; it is safe to be one hundred percent authentically you.

Let me go first with my authentic truth at this moment. I've said it before I'm going to say it again, *"I don't feel like I belong here, writing a leadership book. I don't feel like I'm a leader. I've never called myself a leader."*

But, let me ask you, "What is a leader? Does the old version of what a leader is still work? Does it make sense? Who are we expecting to lead us and where are they leading?" As I sit with these questions, I see leaders everywhere taking paths completely detached from the collective heart. Over time, we have stopped leading from our hearts and we focus on everything else. This is how we got away from leadership in its truest form.

#@&%!!$%$!! What is happening? My mind is exploding as I write this.

When I was a child, leaders weren't called from the inside. In our farming community, they were built from the outside. You were chosen for leadership and then you were groomed by those leaders who chose you. You were taught to follow a structure and how to play a part. *I never believed that everyone could be a leader.*

Let's tap into this idea and consider: do you want to be led by someone who was groomed and taught to follow particular rules? I'm struggling to understand why I accepted this process for so long. I think it's because I *didn't* accept it, *I just didn't question it.* I understood that it was true even if it didn't make sense. That's how life was and I had to learn to live within the construct. *I believed leaders had to be special and I wasn't special.*

Through my process of healing and growing, I've learned that we don't always see our programmed ideas until we have to face our conditioned beliefs. *Here I am, again, completely blindsided by my programmed ideas!* I'm so excited to be shifting these ideas for myself! I'm sitting here wondering how I ever thought this idea was OK. But then I think, I never did, I just didn't know how to change it. I've always admired leaders who broke the rules. I looked up to leaders like Jesus, Gandhi, Mother Teresa, and Martin Luther King, Jr.

Who models leadership for you and who you want to be?

As I consider the leaders that I connect to these ideas dropped in about the thread that connected them:

1. A true leader doesn't just start walking and hope you'll follow: They walk. They forge the path. They walk back, find you along the way, and show you who they are. They meet you where you are, and allow you to decide how to go forward.
2. A true leader doesn't lead through fear and judgment and doesn't need to make you feel small to show you how big they are. A true, heart-centered leader knows and sees that all of us

are already leaders in our own right. They encourage all of us to be our best selves, in this now.
3. A leader goes first. They follow the call, no matter where they are led.

A leader goes first, was the phrase that finally got me to commit to being on this journey. I used to say that I "took the road less traveled," but now I know, I was making my own road. It wasn't that it was less traveled, it was that I was forging a new road for myself, and for you. In those simple words, I finally saw myself as the leader that I've always been. I'm not a leader because I was groomed, but because I listened to the call that lives inside me. I am following my own path because it's where I want to go, not because I hope people will follow me. I am a compass and my needle continues to point me on paths where I go first! I make my own rules. I show up authentically and uniquely create a new way. I'm not a leader because I was chosen, I'm a leader because I am me. You get to be a leader too if you feel the call: *do you desire to go first?*

So, let me go first: "*I AM A LEADER.*

I am here to forge a path to a new way of being.

I am a healer who is holding space for people to heal in.

I am here to create space for you to be the most authentic version of you."

The path I'm forging is about taking up authentic space and thriving in your authenticity. It's about loving yourself just as you are. I remember writing a poem in fourth grade about wanting to be loved for being myself. It was about not wanting to change or shrink to be what you needed to be. I was nine years old and I already possessed a desire for my authentic self to be completely accepted. (Looking back, I also understood that at that moment in my life it wasn't possible.)

Let me tell you another anecdote about my early understanding. In the second grade, I was completely smitten with a boy. I wanted him to be my boyfriend and this feeling lingered within me for *four years*.

Finally, in sixth grade, he said he'd be my boyfriend and I should meet him at the football game. I was so naive, I thought he actually liked me. I was so excited; my dreams were finally coming true! Friday night arrived and as we sat next to each other I could feel his friends watching us. I was shy and when he asked me to go for a walk and tried to hold my hand, I had this feeling that I was about to be the butt of a big joke. I pulled my hand back so fast that he was shocked. He didn't understand why I wouldn't want to hold his hand because he knew I'd liked him for so long. Something inside me knew that his intentions were not authentic or for my greatest good! Needless to say, he "broke up" with me and walked away. This moment showed my younger self that my authentic self wasn't wanted or welcomed: I was crushed on all accounts.

These two memories have infused my journey. The essence of the poem I wrote as a nine year old has lived inside me, urging me forward, and calling me home. My yearning to be loved has always been followed by the stark reality that I experienced time and time again: that my authentic truth wasn't accepted. It was a battle inside me for most of my life—*how can I be me enough to pacify myself but "her" enough to pacify the world?*

As my soul awakened, I began to understand just how many survival walls I had built to pacify my true authentic pieces. The walls weren't built in response to wanting to keep the world out, but rather, wanting to keep all of me inside. I wanted to preserve as much of myself as possible. Deep down I understood that I would be called to awaken to my authentic truth and I wanted to preserve as much of me as possible. I understood exactly what the world was doing to me, and to all of us: the world was attempting to groom us into their idea of leaders and followers.

This was a successful process, so why deviate from a process that works?

In fifth grade I was at piano lessons and I saw the book, *The Giver,* on my teacher's shelf. I borrowed her book and I remember having a clear understanding of what I was doing in this world. I remember feeling a little less alone. I remember thinking, "This is my purpose: I'm here to break the rules. I'm here to hold wisdom and memories, and share them with the world, and help the world awaken too." I had forgotten this knowing, even though I remember reading the book and loving it. I had forgotten what it had shown me. I'm so grateful for this journey and that it helped me remember! I've always known my purpose was about awakening authentic truth.

Fast forward a few decades to when I finally realized I wasn't interested in pacifying myself anymore or pleasing the world. I finally claimed who I was: I AM ALYSEMARIE. I won't be dimmed by me or by anyone else, that isn't authentically who I am.

My parents named me AlyseMarie, but called me Aly. I always wanted to be AlyseMarie. Through the years, I tried to claim that name, *my name*, but I always ended up falling back on Aly because it was easier for everyone else. I'm no longer interested in making my name easy for you. For a long time, I'd be happy if you called me anything at all. Not any more. I'm claiming the truest most authentic version of my being and her name is AlyseMarie. It's nice to meet you.

Now, tell me, what's the truest most authentic version of you? That's who I want to know. That's who I'm forging this path for.

It has always been about the magic of the journey, so let's talk about the epic part of this journey that led me to writing these pages. One year ago, I heard about multi-author books for the first time. I read every post. I even sent it to friends who I thought were a "good fit" for writing a book. Then, the publisher said to me, "What about you? I feel *you* in this space. Do you want to write in this book?" I was taken aback. I was honored. I was scared. I was unsure. I was shocked. She wanted me? This was another chapter of my journey, of embracing my authentic truth and forging the way for you, too.

For a few months, Spirit had been nudging me to coach myself. Each time I replied, "I can't. I don't know how. What do I even know? I can't do this alone. I need someone to show me the way." So, my doubts and I pushed forward doing the same things we had been doing and hoping everything would work itself out. Time passed and again Spirit beckoned, "AlyseMarie, coach yourself, listen to yourself. Heal yourself." And, again stubbornly, I replied, "I CANNOT." Shortly thereafter, co-authoring these books entered my awareness and my journey began. I remembered Jesus telling me to share my story and Mary Magdalene showing me I was worthy. In the words of my first chapter all the cosmic pieces start to align and this new way forward was revealed.

Five books later, here I am, using my words, my channel, and my artistry to heal myself. This isn't me telling you that multi-author books are *the way*, this is me offering you space to go first. This is me encouraging you to forge your own path. This is me celebrating you choosing your heart's way, showing you that your way is your own, and it's the right way, even when it feels a little bit wrong. This is me telling you that you get to decide, you get to choose, you get to be the one who says, "Yes." Oh, that is important! Saying yes and giving yourself permission to choose whatever is calling you, even when it feels uncomfortable is important. Don't forget that you get to meet your edges, you get to choose the uncomfortable thing, if that's where your heart is centered.

There is a beautiful and magical journey waiting for you just beyond the horizon of what you feel is possible. So, go ahead, *go first.* Dream big. Take the journey to whatever authentic truth you seek.

For me? This chapter has been an epic journey all in itself. I started out not even thinking I was a leader, feeling like I didn't belong, struggling to find the words and the way. But, as I sit here wrapping it all up, I can proudly say, I'm a leader. I'm fully heart centered. I did the hard thing: I went first and I came back again because I wanted to. I needed to walk the journey, then turn around and walk it again. I no longer accept anything about myself that isn't my complete authentic truth.

My authentic truth is this: I am a way-shower. I was forged out of stardust with a mastery of anything that fills my heart with joy. I was designed to be special, to shine so brightly that I light the way for everyone seeking to find their own way.

Claiming this authentic truth hasn't been easy. For a long time, I believed that it needed to be difficult, that I needed to work hard to be worthy. Yet, when I fully surrendered to my truth, to my purpose, to the authentic nature of who I was, my truth arrived with ease and beautiful grace. I met the brave little girl inside me and asked her to remind me of who I was. She looked me dead in the eyes and said, "OK, but you have to go first. I can't show you the way. You have to do it and when it's over, you'll know you went the right way because I'll be there next to you. Now go. Find your way back to you. That's how you truly lead…it's all in the journey."

ALYSEMARIE GALLAGHER WARREN

AlyseMarie Gallagher Warren is a Master healer and the go-to "spiritual sidekick" for high level leaders. She helps high achieving women who have created 6 & 7 figure businesses, to create safe spaces to rest, heal and process their success. AlyseMarie's work is rooted in her connection to Mary Magdalene to provide intuitive guidance while her connection to Mother Gaia allows her to be the grounded, spiritual confidant. AlyseMarie is an Executive Chef in Chicago and lives in a cute eclectic bungalow with her artist husband, Spence, and their cat Kramer.

Website: www.alysemariewarren.com

Instagram: @i.am.alysemarie

Facebook: AlyseMarie Gallagher Warren

Email: Alysemarie@channeledpathways.com

LEADING WITH LOVE

On the day of my 70th birthday, I spent the most beautiful and promising time of the day, dawn, staring at the ocean. Studying what seemed to be the calmness of the water miles from the shore, juxtaposed to the waves crashing at my feet. Marveling at the ocean's infinite vastness, I wondered about all the creatures that called the waters their home–species known and unknown. Silently reflecting on my own journey and giving thanks for my life and for my family. During this reflection I wondered what credentials and expertise I had to write a chapter in a book about heart-centered leadership. I thought about the three greatest compliments I received from people that I had been blessed to work with. The first came nearly thirty years ago at a 'going away' celebration for me upon my leaving a leadership position in a large, state bureaucratic organization. During the midst of this gathering, an employee that I supervised came up to me to say that I was the "soul of the organization." This organization, like many other bureaucracies, tended to be impersonal, bound by strict rules and procedures, and conservative in exploring and encouraging ideas and innovation by members of its staff. For me, the compliment meant that I had existed and succeeded in an organization while not conforming to the 'group think' concept of leadership. Years later, even to today, I often visit this idea to remind myself that I can be in an environment and a society, without being of that environment or mind set.

The second compliment also came from an employee when we were discussing an annual performance appraisal. Following the discussion, where we worked together to identify strengths, areas for improvement, the goals the employees wanted to achieve, and the support and resources needed to expand opportunities and ideas, she said to me: "thank you for leading with love." In the center of discussing hard topics about improvement, she was saying to me that even in the midst of having to address her own performance shortcomings, the conversation was conducted with kindness and accountability, with support and autonomy, and encouraging bold action coupled with critical thinking.

The most recent compliment came when a dear friend, whose kinship I share in our work for a more just and loving community, wrote to me from miles away to say: "I find myself thinking about the mentors who have made an impact in my life and you have been on my mind. I hope to emulate your incredibly caring, strategic, genuine coaching, mentoring, and capacity building."

So, as I pondered writing this chapter on leadership, I thought of the qualities that others saw in me. That is, my connection to the Universe and the true power that resides there. I was reminded that love can overcome any adversity and transform lives, communities and the world, and that we all have a responsibility to love, honor, and care for one another.

When I became Chief Executive Officer of a nonprofit organization some three years ago, I thought deeply about accepting the position. This was not a position within the hierarchy of the organization that I sought or wanted to pursue. Yet, years before I was offered this position, I intuitively knew that I would one day occupy this space. And then, like the collapse of Enron, what was seen as improbable happened. The founder and longtime leader transitioned out of the organization, and being the next in line, I was offered the position. While I had been with the organization for many years, my concern was not fear of succeeding in the job, despite the fact that I knew there would be significant challenges facing the organization in the days to come. Rather, having evaded this level of leadership and responsibility during my career, choosing to work in anonymity behind the scenes, and satisfied with the monetary rewards of lesser positions, the question I struggled with was what value would I bring to the organization, to the people who work here, and to the people and communities we served. Was the organization ready for the only type of leadership I could in good conscience provide? A style of leadership that I was not willing to compromise. I struggled with this because everything in the world says that in order to succeed in leading organizations you must be aggressive, competitive, impersonal, motivated by the need to get more, that there was no place for kindness and love, and that only external power mattered. I was not sure that there was a place for my leadership in such a world—even in a nonprofit organization.

But then I thought, what if I could bring my style of leadership to the organization? What if I could model the power of such leadership to others? What if others could see and learn from my example that you do not have to forsake time tested and universal values and principles to have true, transformational success? And, so my thoughts in accepting the position was that maybe, just maybe the story that I might get to tell and bear witness to one day would be how to lead through collaboration and not competition. A story of leading from the power of internal connectedness, rather than the illusion of external power. A story of leading from gratefulness, respect, and reverence for others rather than aggressiveness, arrogance, and ego. A story of leading from love and righteous intention rather than selfishness, greed, and exclusiveness. I believed that leading in this manner can conquer any challenge and adversity, can solve any problem, and create a life, a community and a world filled with good life outcomes for all. With this as my mission, I decided to give it a try.

Collaboration. Helping to forge a path is not about who is out front clearing the pathway, it is about the group moving together–someone at every vantage point–in front, behind, side-to-side, from every strategic angle, no one point-of-view is more important than the other. A threat can come from anywhere, just like an opportunity or an idea can fall like rain on everyone in the group. All in the group, working in unison with the focus on one goal, depending on the other, believing that they can do anything.

So, I strive to create a culture and environment that lets everyone who works within the organization know that I might be CEO, but that I am no more important than each of them. I repeat often that we are only limited by not working as one body and by not imagining what power we possess to create magnificent opportunities for the people we serve and, in the process, the intrinsic byproduct of discovering joy in our own lives. It is not an easy thing to get everyone to fully believe or accept that such a concept can be realized. Yes, at times I feel like John the Baptist, preaching in the wilderness. But I believe that with every amazing feat we accomplish as an organization, that with every individual risk and bold action they take and find support and encouragement, and that they will see how the people they touch and serve benefit by their action.

In the nonprofit arena, I do not see competition with the other roughly 1.8 million registered nonprofit organizations in the United States. There is more than enough suffering in my community and in the world that no one organization will be able to fill. So, I actively look for opportunities to partner with other organizations, to collaborate on ideas and new programs, and to reward and support other organizations to build their capacity. When I think of collaboration, I believe that to have true, transformational, and sustaining significance it takes all of us working together. And that is not just for nonprofit organizations, I believe it to be true for every aspect of our society and the world. Like the group, Funkadelic sings in, "One Nation Under a Groove" we have the chance to "dance our way out of our constrictions" and "nothing can stop us…".

Internal Connectedness. From the time I was a child, around the age of six, I felt a centering connection to a universal God. Maybe it came from sitting in a circle with my mother, grandmothers, and other 'sisters' from the Baptist Church that my family were members of. This 'mission' circle met weekly and I joined in many of these meetings–mostly because they always had refreshments and treats following the discussion. But there in that circle, sitting beside Sister Lee, the oldest member of the church, along with my participation in every activity that took place at my church, the foundation was laid and I knew without a doubt that I was surrounded and supported by a loving and enduring Force, that would always be in love with me, no matter what. And while over the course of my life, I questioned, pleaded, criticized, the 'why' of the uncertainties, pain, and adversities in my life, I never doubted that amazing love, or that I was not alone, and that the power that resides in the Force therefore resides in me. This is not for agreement and debate. It just is and it drives every intention I have to try and do good in every aspect of my life.

So, whatever strategic plans, personnel issues, or the ongoing fundraising challenges that face the organization, no decisions or actions are taken without consideration of the ancient principles of love, equality and opportunity for all, mercy, and the greater good.

Gratefulness, Respect, and Reverence. I do not think that you can have an internal connectedness to God and this universe and not practice gratefulness, respect, and reverence. What do I find to be grateful for as a leader? First, I am grateful to work with a group of talented and committed individuals that show up every day to perform individual acts of service that most people will never know of their individual contributions. Individuals who work with people who are often ignored in our society, people with drug addictions, experiencing homelessness, without access to health care coverage, and people who are disproportionately affected by the criminal justice system, to just name the tip of the challenges they face daily. We may understand that drug addiction is a problem, but to truly understand the magnitude of what these champions face, and its effect on individuals, you have to look deeper into the shadow like the young girl whose mother suffers from drug addiction and 'pimps' her out to feed and pay for her addiction; or the young boy who is bullied and teased at school because other neighborhood children have witnessed his mother have sex in a car on a public street for all to see; or how a family was evicted from their apartment because an adult daughter brought her mother to live with her because of her mother's health disability and needed her care, resulting in a family of four living in a truck. This is the work we do. How can you not be grateful to work with champions that show up each day to try and help others? How can you not be grateful that the adversities experienced by so many people in this world have spared you and your family? How can you not be grateful that you have an opportunity to play a small role in alleviating some of the suffering?

From the early days of sitting in the mission circle, I always felt that whatever the circumstances of the other, we were all the same, one humanity on one planet together; our common humanity and kinship makes us all worthy of respect. My definition of respect is not one where you give respect because you have a sense of admiration for something that someone accomplished. Although the truth be told, if we take the time to look further than a person's occupation, physical appearance, or socioeconomic status we would find a deep sense of admiration for how most people go about their daily life meeting challenges and struggles with courage and grace. I remember sitting in a crowded airport restaurant and there was only one attendant taking orders and serving guests. I sat and observed her serve people who were in a hurry to make a flight, people from various backgrounds and cultures, and people impatient and exasperated from the stress of travel. She moved through the crowd, going from table to table with grace and ease. Taking orders without any device to make note of the orders, greeting people with a warm smile that was not deterred by the customer's apparent irritation. Orders came out on time, everyone received what they ordered, and patrons were checked on regularly to see if they needed anything. I marveled at the skills that it took to handle that restaurant crowd. I also thought about the people I had met in my life–influential people, high ranking public officials, leaders of large corporations, people from all walks and fields of life, and I knew that they possess no more special skills than this one, Black woman handling this restaurant. In fact, many did not measure up to her skills. Yet here she was serving others in an airport restaurant.

My respect is not just for our common humanity, but also for the fact that the "least among us" have been endowed with the same abilities, if not the opportunities, as so many others that are admired for their skills and talents. I lead a black-founded, black-led organization and we dare to do our work every day in the midst of the struggle for equity. The organization knows well how black-led organizations are seen as less trusted and don't have the connections and access to philanthropic leaders. Even if their organization has found innovative ways to double the organization's budget in two years, expand programs to fill gaps and serve more people, has evidence-based data to demonstrate outcomes, and is creating a gateway to build the capacity of other grassroots, community-based organizations.

Just like all of us living on this planet, an organization is a collective group, all sharing a common kinship, a community of people with differences and difficulties. What could we accomplish–could we cure diseases, or end world hunger, or end poverty–if we appreciated and was grateful for opportunities to enrich the lives of others, if we respected all of us, and if we bowed in reverence to all we meet and all that this planet offers to each of us? That is the journey I set out on to find the answers to my questions.

Love. The common theme of this writing is that all things begin with love. When you are guided by love for all mankind, love for an organization, or love for the people you serve, then your actions and intentions will align with love. Love and righteous intention will help you chart a course that may be rocky, foreboding, and uncertain; that may be filled with twists, turns, and disappointment; and days where you barely hold on. Leading in love is not easy, especially in a world where everything says and reinforces that you are on the wrong path, a world that seeks to disconnect us from one another rather than connect us. Where others say love is a weakness, I believe it to be our greatest strength. Where others say you cannot measure love or its impact. I say love can be observed, can move people into action, and that people are transformed by love. So, my work is grounded in heart-centered love. I hope to lead in love and let the light of love shine my way and the way for others.

HELEN STAGG

Helen Stagg is Chief Executive Officer of Change Happens, a community-based social service organization in Houston, Texas. She is responsible for operational planning and management, program operations and oversight, addressing strategic organizational issues, human resources planning and management, financial planning and management, and community relations/advocacy. Ms. Stagg received a Bachelor of Arts degree from Texas A&M University, Commerce, and a Masters in Social Work from the University of Houston, Graduate College of Social Work. She is also an Internationally Certified Prevention Specialist. Ms. Stagg serves on the board of the Texas Association of Substance Abuse Programs, the Greater Houston Healthy Marriage Coalition, and the Advisory Board of the University of Houston's Health Research Institute. Ms. Stagg has been featured in a documentary commissioned by The Robert Wood Johnson Foundation, Promise Story: "Empowering Community Health." Ms. Stagg is also an adjunct professor at the University of Houston Clear Lake and University of Houston Graduate College of Social Work.

Website: www.changehappenstx.org

Email: hstagg@changehappenstx.org

MY JOURNEY TO BECOMING A SECURELY-ATTACHED LEADER

"Develop enough courage so that you can stand up for yourself, and then stand up for somebody else."

- Maya Angelou

For most of my youth and young adulthood, I considered myself a 'people pleaser'. I grew up in rural Minnesota, among the descendants of Scandinavian and German immigrants. Stoic yet kind, hospitable, hard-working people. People who go out of their way to help a friend, and always have a casserole ready to whip up for visitors or a neighbor in need.

The message I received from my family and community was, "always be kind and respectful, use your manners, and don't cause trouble." Though these were intended to be positive messages, I internalized them to mean I'd better not rock the boat, and that if I did something to upset someone, there must be something wrong with me.

I felt responsible for the feelings of others. In my twenties, I saw this people-pleasing mentality impact romantic relationships and friendships. I felt insecure and unworthy of love if I didn't 'make others happy.' I was anxiously-attached and I distanced myself from others. Professionally, my people-pleasing tendencies held me back countless times from pursuing my passions and dreams, for fear that I'd let someone down and ultimately, be unlovable.

It took several years into my career as a therapist to understand and accept that I am not responsible for others, only for myself: my actions, reactions, and intentions. We can only focus on approaching others with authenticity and positive intent. And our ability to do so depends on the relationship we have with ourselves.

For me it's been a lifelong journey towards a secure relationship with myself (more on this below). This includes the ability to put my feelings and needs first and know this is not selfish but necessary if I want to have a positive impact on others. This quote above by Maya Angelou has always been one of my favorites. When we demonstrate self-respect and engage in self-advocacy, we can then do so for others, and more importantly, model this for those we lead.

Simply put, our attachment style is our way of relating to others in close relationships. John Bowlby, one of the pioneers of attachment research and theory, suggests that our attachment style is formed from our experiences with our primary caregivers in infancy and early childhood. We either learn that we can trust and rely on others and that deep connections feel safe (a secure attachment), or that we must protect ourselves in some way, and have difficulty connecting to and relying on others (an insecure attachment).

Another pioneer in the world of psychology, Erik Erikson, identified stages of psychosocial development across the lifespan which inform our personality and sense of self. The first stage in infancy, 'basic trust versus mistrust', is when we begin to form our opinions about the world around us: is it safe or unsafe? This learning takes place within the context of our primary attachment relationships, i.e.: can we rely on our caregivers to meet our basic needs. And those beliefs generalize to the world around us. The next stage which occurs in toddlerhood, 'autonomy versus shame and doubt', is where we begin to form the relationship with the self. If independence is encouraged to a healthy degree, we begin to build confidence in our abilities and security within ourselves.

John Bowlby's and Erik Erikson's work combined say everything about the importance of those early experiences in relationships, and how we begin to form our core beliefs, sense of self, and attachment with the self.

All relationships are a mirror of the relationship we have with ourselves (i.e., our own *attachment* style). In other words, the way we experience ourselves and our core beliefs about ourselves are projected into the world and manifested in our experiences with others. When we feel insecure and doubt ourselves and our worth, feeling as though we're not enough, we play out these themes in relationships. This can show up in the form of a self-fulfilling prophecy. For example, if we fear rejection, we might avoid connection with others. When someone invites us to a social event, we initially say yes, feeling excited about new potential friendships and the feeling of belonging. However, at the last minute, that inner critic shows up and says "what if you say something dumb and they think you're awkward; what if they don't like you?", and we make an excuse and bail on the plans. We flake out enough and that person stops inviting us altogether, only reinforcing our fear of rejection.

On the other hand, when we practice self-acceptance and self-compassion, and we truly believe we are enough no matter what, we're able to approach others genuinely and openly, with acceptance, compassion, and love. And we get to receive those gifts back from others, because we believe we're worthy. If we're rejected in some way, we're able to practice self-kindness and know we are enough regardless of what others may think.

When we take things personally or internalize the opinions of others, naturally our defenses go up. When our guard is up, it's difficult to connect in genuine and meaningful ways. We engage in unhelpful protective mechanisms, which impacts our personal and professional connections. However as leaders we are required to deeply connect with and truly see and hear those we lead. We're asked to practice genuine openness and vulnerability. And this ability to connect with others in meaningful ways stems from our ability to deeply connect with ourselves.

Relationships are at the core of Heart-Centered Leadership. And it starts with the relationship the leader has with oneself. Heart-Centered Leadership means approaching leadership from a securely-attached place in which we remove fears and ego and lead with love, compassion, and trust. It means reframing the way we approach holding success, a team, and a community. Knowing your attachment style. Acknowledging whatever privilege and biases we hold. It involves embracing our humanness, and a willingness to be accountable to and vulnerable about our own challenges.

Secure attachment at its core is about the relationship with the self. The essence of secure attachment is self-acceptance and a deep knowing of worth. It means feeling self-contented, and being aware of and able to express feelings and needs assertively. It manifests in the ability to connect genuinely with others, put trust and faith in others, and the capacity to build deep, meaningful, long-lasting relationships.

When I was a kid and a midwest girl navigating her twenties, my attachment style was a combination of secure and anxious (insecure). I was considered 'sensitive' as a child because of my intense emotions, as well as my high level of awareness of and empathy for the experiences of others. My mother called me her "tender heart." And in my friend groups, I loved to listen to the 'problems' of others. I often found myself in a mediator position with 'drama' between friends. When I was a senior in high school, I took my first Psychology class, and was hooked. Today, I'm a therapist, coach, supervisor, consultant, and CEO of a group mental health practice. In a nutshell: I help individuals connect with themselves.

So I became a therapist. It was perfect because since childhood, I've been obsessed with personal growth, and the idea of helping others.

MY JOURNEY TO BECOMING A SECURELY-ATTACHED LEADER

I've always been fascinated with psychology, lifespan development, and the human mind. I believe I was put on this earth to be the best human I can be, and to help others do the same. I'm not sure if my personal growth obsession is innate, or something that comes from my experiences as an athlete growing up and being coached by my father, or even having a mother who instilled in me things like "attitude is everything." It was likely a combination of all three.

However, the story of being a people pleaser, nervous of disrupting, hesitant to ruffle feathers doesn't end at my Psychology degree. While the secure attachment style is the most common type of attachment in western society and research suggests that around 66% of the US population is securely attached, cultivating a secure attachment isn't innate (Keller, 2018). I believe attachment style is fluid. Our attachment style moves toward security the more we work on the relationship we have with ourselves. For me, securely attaching has been a process that evolved and shifted throughout my life.

Becoming a business owner and leader in my field has been a tremendous opportunity for personal growth and securely attaching to myself. It hasn't always been a smooth road, and my people-pleasing tendencies have been challenged countless times. I've had to learn how to let go of the fear of disappointing others and accept that I can't make everyone happy. I've also had to learn how to put my full trust and faith in others in order to delegate and grow the business. My "do-it-all and save-the-world" mentality has been extremely difficult to release, as I've learned to feel safe without a need for control. I've felt the discomfort of 'imposter syndrome' on a regular basis. I've been humbled over and over again through the many mistakes I've made along the way. And I still have so much to learn. What it's come down to is my ability to practice self-acceptance, self-compassion, and believe in myself to overcome any obstacles. And what's made these practices possible is connecting with those I lead in meaningful ways, asking for help, and empowering others. Loving myself and feeling secure within myself allows me to pour my love and energy into those I lead.

Developing a secure attachment style helps us trust in the greater good by trusting in the good of others. It dissolves our need to be right, or please others. Someone wise once taught me about the concept of "assuming positive intent." When we are able to put our trust in others and their intentions, we remove ourselves from a fear-based, victim mentality. We move into a place of ownership and empowerment, for ourselves and others.

I believe that a healthy relationship with oneself is key to well-being, happiness, and success in life. From this foundation, individuals experience improvement and increased satisfaction in all areas of life, including but not limited to: emotional well-being, relationships, career, health and wellness, leisure, spirituality and purpose, and overall happiness and contentment in life. I recently heard Will Smith say, "Happiness is peace." From my perspective, security leads us to peace. The more secure we feel within ourselves and in our interactions with others, the more we can experience this inner peace.

I also believe that resilience is key for this journey of well-being, which is why the name of my business is Center for Resilience Strategies. We focus on supporting clients as they increase emotional intelligence and resilience, foster healthy coping strategies and communication skills, enrich their relationships, and adopt healthy life habits.

As leaders, our ability to cultivate secure attachment leads to more resilient relationships, teams, companies, and communities. So much is how we view ourselves and others.

What does securely-attached leadership look like? As mentioned above, the core is about self-awareness and a healthy relationship with oneself. This includes a sense of self-worth, overall self-acceptance, and the ability to practice self-kindness, self-compassion, and self-respect. A securely-attached leader knows one's strengths, challenges, limits, needed areas of growth, and sees oneself as capable and resilient. This leader has healthy boundaries and is able to communicate needs effectively. This leader is willing to model being human and makes mistakes without self-criticism or judgment. They're willing to be vulnerable. A securely-attached leader believes in oneself to lead and make an impact. They see their own worth, what they can offer others, and what they can contribute to society. This leader overall has a sense of optimism and hope.

Externally, a securely-attached leader leads from a place of love. This leader has the ability to recognize, honor, and appreciate strengths in others, and encourage growth in challenging areas in a loving, compassionate, encouraging manner. They do not see others as threatening. This leader believes in others; they put trust and faith in others, delegate, rely on others, and ultimately encourage others to shine and succeed. A securely-attached leader possesses a collaborative nature and gives direct yet productive feedback. Holds high standards for self and others, yet approaches expectations from a supportive, understanding, compassionate, flexible place. Empowers staff versus doing it for them. Ability to hold space for others and not 'take on' the problems of others. Active listening skills. Accepts what they cannot change and what they cannot control. Appreciates growth, improvement, evolution. Growth mindset. Perspective of gratitude. Appreciates and honors differences in relationships. Is willing to acknowledge privilege and biases. Willingness to be a student and learn from others, just as much if not more than being a teacher.

So how does secure attachment lead to resilience?

Resilience is the ability to recover from a challenge or hardship and return to a 'baseline' state of functioning efficiently and effectively. Some say it means to 'bounce back' from something. To me resilience is about having the skills necessary to not only recover, but become better, after a difficult experience. I don't want to just bounce back, I want to evolve. As leaders we must be willing to use failures, setbacks, rejections, and disappointments to learn and improve.

Securely attached individuals, and those we'd consider having a high level of resilience share similar internal narratives. Things like... The world is a generally safe place and I can rely on the support of others... I feel connected to those around me... The world and the people in my life have my back... I've got this... I can get through this... I am capable... I am willing to learn and grow... I am okay... I am enough...

In many ways I approach leadership the way I approach motherhood. I want my children to be healthy and able to cope with and learn from challenges in life--to grow despite hardship, and to feel confident, strong, and brave--to take life by the horns, and to be able to ride every wave in the sea of uncertainty. By empowering others to cultivate secure attachment in oneself, we foster resilience. As leaders and mentors, we can do this for others by...

Connecting with them.

Listening to them.

Encouraging self-reflection and self-awareness.

Fostering self-acceptance and self-compassion.

Teaching problem-solving skills.

Encouraging independent thought.

Teaching and modeling a positive attitude.

Accepting and validating emotions, even fear.

Helping develop healthy coping strategies.

Encouraging well-rounded self-care practices.

Teaching them about and modeling healthy, loving relationships.

Modeling for them that it's okay to be an imperfect human; we all make mistakes.

Instilling perseverance and grit.

Showing them how to take ownership and accountability--to be responsible and hold themselves to a high standard.

Modeling values of honesty, integrity, kindness, compassion, and humility.

Assisting them in identifying their areas of strength and challenges.

Helping them identify their goals and dreams, and supporting those.

Believing in them so that they can believe in themselves.

However...

That's a lot. It's a mountain of things to remember, and a tremendous task. The reality is, we are not responsible for the experiences and choices of others. We can only take ownership over our individual journeys toward secure attachment and resilience. But we can plant the seeds, by showing up from a place of Heart Centered Leadership. I'll end with two more of my favorite Maya Angelou quotes to drive home some encouragement for securely-attached leadership:

> "Do the best you can until you know better. Then when you know better, do better."

> "I learned a long time ago, the wisest thing I can do is be on my own side."

References

https://www.pnas.org/doi/10.1073/pnas.1720325115

ALLISON BRATSCH

Allison Bratsch, Licensed Professional Counselor, is the Founder & CEO of Center for Resilience Strategies (CRS), a community-based counseling and coaching clinic serving the greater Denver, CO area. CRS' mission is to provide accessible, affordable, and effective mental health services to individuals of all ages, couples, and families. Allison leads a team of 25 therapists and 3 administrative support staff. Her passion lies in providing her team with a supportive and empowering space to grow and thrive.

Allison has spent the last 14 years working with children, teens, adults, couples, and families to combat the effects of stress, trauma, mental illness, and more. She's obsessed with personal growth. She believes she was put on this earth to discover her best self, and to help others do the same. Her broader life mission is to change the culture of mental health by inspiring others to make emotional health and wellness a priority.

Website: www.crscounseling.com

Instagram: @crs_counseling

Facebook: @strategiesforresilience

HEART-CENTERED, FEELINGS FOCUSED

To be a heart-centered leader, getting out of your head is crucial.

Starting as early as middle school, I lived my life primarily from my head–analyzing every action, ruminating over every potential outcome of each decision, and stressing myself out by overthinking all that could result from making the 'wrong' one. This head-focused lifestyle unfortunately often led to paralysis and rendered me too afraid to take any action at all. Even though I knew this about myself, it took me some time to realize just how pervasive this deep-seated fear was and how it was affecting all areas of my life. Diving headfirst into the fear, a process that I will describe later in this chapter, was a major turning point in my journey and it was connecting with my body's divine wisdom that helped me realize that I had a profound fear of making a mistake. I had the extreme thought that if I made a wrong decision then the rest of my life would be negatively affected and there would be no way to correct it. To my nervous system, that translated to: making a mistake is catastrophic and I would not be safe.

My young body adapted to this fear by taking on perfectionism, OCD, and an eating disorder that carried into adulthood—all attempts to control aspects of my life. As I began my healing journey and learned about how people adapt to trauma, I realized these were all coping mechanisms that I developed as a result of my parents' divorce, when I felt completely out of control. Once I chose to pay attention to the triggers in my life and dive deep into the underbelly of what was behind those triggers, I learned that my body was storing a lot of repressed emotions from the trauma I experienced growing up. It is my connection to the feelings within my body that now empower me to get out of my head and show up as a heart-centered leader both in my therapy practice and my corporate role.

BACKSTORY

As any child of divorce knows, the time of separation is an emotional one. For me, it happened when I was eight years old and newly living with my mother and younger sister, I had an immense amount of pressure placed upon me to be the "man of the house." This meant being a role model to my sister, trying to manage my father's rage, and, most impactful of all, being my mother's surrogate emotional spouse. The clinical term for the dynamic with my mother is covert incest and it arises when a parent uses a child to meet their needs. This trauma had lasting effects on my ability to connect with my feelings and with others in a healthy way. If you want to learn more about this type of trauma, I recommend looking up covert incest by psychologist Ken Adams.

I had to disconnect from my feelings to show up as the perfect son. For example when I felt sad or angry about the circumstances and would try to express that, I was told "you have to get over it, things happen." Essentially I was taught that my feelings were not as important as my parents' and so I learned to bury my emotions to cope. What I really needed was support. I needed to be told that it was okay to play, to be a kid, and that I wasn't responsible for managing my parents' emotions. But to me, I couldn't be a kid. This was a matter of survival. I felt that if I didn't grow up quickly and support my struggling mother, then she wouldn't be able to manage, and we'd end up living on the street—a fear that she often voiced. How do you think hearing this supports a developing brain? Spoiler: it doesn't.

I developed people pleasing tendencies and suppression of my emotions that carried over into all relationships in my life. I became very analytical and in my head. I recall thinking "If I can just figure everything out, then I'll be successful." This was my mantra for years and I realized later that what I was really saying was "Once I figure everything out, I'll be safe."

TWO JOES

This desire for success/safety is what drove my ambition and culminated in a job I had pedestalized: software consulting. A couple of years into working at this consulting firm I realized I had 'arrived' at that place I'd been dreaming of since I was a child, on paper anyway. I had the salary, the prestigious job, moved to the beautiful state of Colorado with my wife, and yet I still felt something was missing. Why wasn't I more fulfilled?

It was during a plant medicine experience in 2018 when I had the idea to be a psychedelic guide and for the first time, I felt connected to something truly purpose-driven. Being cared for in a safe container and supported by others during my experience was a defining moment in my life because for the first time, I saw what it looked like to work in a way that could help others in a meaningful way. The role of a psychedelic guide is to create a safe space for the client to have their experience. I later became credentialed in Mindfulness-Based Psychedelic Therapy with a specialty in Cannabis-Assisted Psychedelic Therapy and started a business facilitating journeys for clients in 1-on-1 and group settings. Holding space for others is a significant part of my calling in this life and I am immensely grateful to be living out this purpose. Finally, I found something that fulfilled me.

At the time of writing this, I am both a psychedelic therapist and a manager at a consulting firm. For a long time, how I showed up in each of these roles was very different from one another. In my therapy practice, I focus on creating a container where clients' nervous systems can feel deeply safe and they can process any emotions that arise. I lead with my heart so they can connect to theirs.

As a manager in my firm, however, it had been a different story. I once received feedback from a superior that I was coming off harsh to my peers. After reflecting on my experience, I could see that I was not showing up in a heart-centered way. Even though I was leading with my heart with my clients, when it came to my corporate job, I would put on the mask of someone I didn't like. My childhood trauma was informing how I was engaging in this job. I thought that to thrive in that environment I had to bury how I was feeling—"get over it" and do the job in order to be successful/safe. This resulted in resentment towards the job and I was taking it out on my peers. I realized I was giving myself permission to be my authentic self within my therapy practice but letting the stories in my head run the show in my corporate life.

I was living in dissonance and realized if I was to fully embody my purpose and give my gifts to the world, there could no longer be "Corporate Joe" and "Therapist Joe," but instead I would need to bring all of me to every aspect of my life. I needed to live from my heart and not my head. Since I was managing a team, it was more important than ever to not only do my job well, but to empower and enable others to rise up and embody their highest selves.

Bringing all of me to every aspect of life and leading with my heart requires mindfulness of the sensations and emotions in my body, self-exploration, humility, practice, and acceptance. My compass throughout this journey is my feelings, pointing me in the direction of my soul's calling.

FROM THOUGHTS TO FEELINGS

I envision a world where all leaders are heart-centered and express their authentic selves while being in harmony with self-limiting thoughts. While self-limiting thoughts may never completely go away, it's our relationship to them that influences how we move forward. When I came to terms with the notion that these thoughts may never leave, it freed me from the pressure of trying to be perfect. There is power in noticing the thoughts, allowing them without attachment, and then taking the action that feels most aligned regardless of what the thoughts are saying. This is living from the heart—taking action that feels inspired and lights you up. Living this way empowers others to embrace their authentic selves and share their unique gifts with the world. Once thoughts are in the driver seat, that's when the head takes over.

Thoughts are just that—thoughts. They are not truths and with awareness, they don't need to dictate your actions. They only have as much meaning as you assign to them. For example, having the thought that you can't do something doesn't mean that you can't do it. When you're feeling that you want to take action but have fear around it, I invite you to explore the fear. Dig into what that fear is rooted in. Either with a partner who you feel safe with or journaling to yourself, talk through all the thoughts and emotions that you notice around the fear. Don't hold back. Voice the fear, judgment, shame, guilt, and any other emotions. No feelings are bad or wrong and all feelings are valid. By voicing your feelings, they lose the power they have over you.

HEART-CENTERED PRACTICES

To those who want to cultivate more heart-centered living, I recommend strengthening your connection to your emotions. The stronger that connection is, the more in tune you are to your soul-aligned success. To me, soul-aligned success means embodying a life of harmony between what lights you up, what the world needs, and what supports your path. To show up as a heart-centered leader, you must bring your whole self everyday.

Below are practices I leverage both when supporting clients and when managing my team at my consulting firm. Helping others become more self-aware and in tune with their feelings is ultimately what supports them in realizing their vision.

Ask yourself the following questions next time you're feeling a strong emotion:

1. What am I feeling?
2. How are these feelings familiar?
3. Am I feeling this feeling in any other areas of my life?
4. When is the earliest memory I have of feeling this way?
5. What do I need right now?

Exploring these questions is the emotional equivalent of working out at the gym. At the gym, you focus on the action of lifting the weight and the more you do it, the stronger your muscles get and the easier it becomes. Exploring your fears and asking these questions is growing the muscle of connecting to your emotions. There isn't necessarily something to do with the answers to the questions. The intention is to bring awareness to the feelings your body is experiencing.

Question #5 might be particularly difficult to connect to when you're first starting out. Learning what your unique needs are requires time, education, and exploration. You can find a list of universal human needs by searching online for the communication approach of Nonviolent Communication. This approach to communication assumes all humans have basic needs and the experience of feelings are the result of these needs either being met or unmet. Maybe you need to hear "it's okay" (need of safety) or "your feelings are valid" (need of being understood) or maybe you need a hug (need for touch). Whatever you need in that moment, give yourself permission to have it and know that it's okay to ask that from a trusted partner or friend, even if that person has nothing to do with whatever feelings have arisen. These words and actions are strategies that help you meet the underlying needs.

Connecting to your emotions is the way to get into your heart but when emotions arise, it can be intense and it can be very challenging to go through the above steps. Knowledge of polyvagal theory can be helpful here. This theory is a construct related to the role of the Autonomic Nervous System (ANS) in emotional regulation and fear response. The sympathetic and parasympathetic nervous system both make up the ANS and it determines which state your body is in—rest/safety, fight/flight, or shut-down. There are visuals online that graphically show these states and it can be helpful to have that chart handy for reference. The next time you're feeling an emotion, I invite you to take a moment to connect to what state your body is in. If you are feeling angry or anxious, you're likely in the fight/flight state. If you're feeling present and grounded, you're likely in the rest/safe state. This is the place where you are most connected to your authentic self and empowered to make decisions that align with your soul. There are tips online on how to move into rest/safety.

Another powerful exercise I suggest is to define your dream self. Who is the person you want to become? While you are doing this, know that there is nothing wrong with the person you are now. Every part of you is perfect—even the judgmental, shameful, or guilty thoughts/voices. You can love yourself as you are now and have an intention for your future self. In fact, you must feel like you are progressing to fully tap into the awesome energy that is life. As Tony Robbins says, progress results from consciously choosing to create a life you love and to me, the first step in choosing that life is getting clear on your dream self.

When envisioning your dream self, think through these questions: How do I want to feel in my body? How would my highest self respond to an annoyance? How would the person I admire show up in the face of adversity? What activities am I doing? How am I spending my time each week? Everyone's answers to these questions will be different. This is an excerpt from my vision of my dream self: "I am the man my younger self wanted to become. I'm leading life from my heart and with passion. My family sees me as a strong capable king and protector who accomplishes any goal he sets."

I also find it helpful to define my vision in the form of guiding principles. They include my values as well as Wills and Won'ts. Here is the template I use, feel free to do this in the way that makes the most sense to you.

Will:

1. Communicate boundaries with compassion
2. Remember that mistakes are okay

Won't:

1. Multi-task, it stresses my ANS
2. Speak sarcastically, it is not being impeccable with my word

I struggled to figure out what my values were since I used to think that if I wasn't already living that value 100% of the time I couldn't authentically claim it as a value. It felt like I was lying. If you have these thoughts, I invite you to allow them without attaching yourself to them and write them down. I don't always follow these successfully but that is why they are my guiding principles and not my rules. I've found by writing these down and claiming them, I have carried through on them most of the time. Set the intention to create a list for yourself and stay curious to the signals that come into your life and write them down as new ones arise. This is a dynamic list and should continue to be updated, feel free to add/remove as it feels right to you.

The point of writing down your values/principles is not to be hard on yourself if you think, act, or speak in a way that isn't in line with them. The point is to set up a structure that reminds you of who you want to become so that when you either A. act in a way that is in line with your values, you can celebrate and feel proud of yourself for taking a step towards the person you are becoming or B. act in a way that is not aligned, you can notice it and explore why you acted that way. Awareness is key and being able to reference your unique values makes awareness easier.

Implementing these practices has helped me reconnect to the emotions within my body that I was disconnected from due to my childhood trauma. I am no longer burying my emotions or trying to figure everything out to be successful/feel safe. Instead I have learned, and continue to learn, to accept and dance with the full spectrum of my emotions while not allowing them to overwhelm me. My relationship with my ANS and my emotions has united the two Joes and I'm more connected with myself and others as a result.

Emotions are the key to connecting with your heart. While the mind is important to figure out how to achieve what your heart is calling you to do, it is when these two energy centers are working in unison, with the heart leading and the head following, that your body is most primed for soul-aligned success. You can do it, the world needs you, and the only way is through your heart. Even when it doesn't feel like it, and it will not always feel like it, remember that you are right where you're supposed to be. Encourage yourself to keep trying, like you would encourage a child. Over and over.

JOE DINARDO

Joe Dinardo is a psychedelic guide, integration coach, and founder of Embodied Healing. He helps curious men and women who desire knowing themselves on a deeper level through cannabis-assisted psychedelic therapy. With curiosity, non-judgement, and compassion he helps spiritual seekers explore how their past experiences may be impacting their lives today, gain new perspectives, connect to self-love, and rediscover the sacredness of the plant ally Cannabis. Certified through the Center for Medicinal Mindfulness, Joe takes a trauma-informed approach to prioritizing safety because he believes when the nervous system is regulated and one feels truly safe, healing is bound to occur. He leverages experience from polyvagal theory, inner child work, and mindfulness practices to live from his heart in all areas of his life including at home with his wife, Chrissy, and two cats, Max and Ollie, as well as in his role as a manager within a consulting firm.

Website: www.embodiedhealingwithjoe.com

UNSTOPPABLE

I was leaping up and down on the bed I shared with my then boyfriend, so happy that I had a diagnosis. I didn't even hear the doctor say, "You'll have this for the rest of your life".

I was so grateful to know I hadn't just made up all of these symptoms. There was something that could explain the uncontrollable weight gain, the debilitating fatigue, the crippling anxiety and terrifying depression, the endless bathroom trips and what seemed like my entire head of hair ending up on the bathroom floor.

I had a diagnosis. Hypothyroidism.

That's all that mattered to me.

And something could be done about it...

Or so I thought.

I followed the instructions, the same way I had with the 'IBS' diagnosis, years earlier. I took the medication as prescribed and I started to feel better. Unfortunately it was short lived. Six months later I was back in the doctor's office convinced I just needed a stronger prescription, like I had with my eye glasses when I was growing up.

Only this time when the doctor got my test results she said, "Your thyroid is fine, there's nothing more I can do for you. I suggest you find an antidepressant".

"A what?", I said, outraged. "The last time I checked my hair wasn't falling out because I was depressed. I've done my research. Would you please run a full thyroid panel to see what is causing the issue and to see if I have the Autoimmune Disease, Hashimoto's?"

"No I won't, you are making things too complicated. Just take your medication."

It was like a slap in the face. I thought my doctor was supposed to help me but she wouldn't do anything except provide medication that wasn't working.

At that moment I knew I'd have to find someone that would listen to me. It was the first time I felt that burning feeling inside. You know the one? That feeling where you just know you have to listen to your intuition and follow it to the ends of the earth to get to your truth. That leadership moment, leadership of your own life. I realized I had a choice. I could stay sick and disempowered OR, I could choose a life by my design filled with vitality and health.

It's probably no surprise, I chose the second option. I fired that doctor and went on a search.

Searching for someone that would listen and care, someone to be a partner with me in my health. That's when I was introduced to Dr. G who was a NYC chiropractor turned Functional Medicine provider. I remember taking the subway all the way up to 181st street on a wish and a pretty strong recommendation from a friend. Walking into his office, I was holding my breath because I just didn't think I could handle being disappointed again. I was so desperate to feel like me again. I would do anything. When I met him, I started to tell him how I was feeling, waiting with bated breath, knowing that any second, he would cut me off and tell me just to take my medication.

Only this time was different. He just let me talk. He was the first medical person to truly listen to me. I talked to him for 90 minutes and walked away with hearts in my eyes because I couldn't believe there was someone out there who would take the time to really hear what I had to say. And beyond just listening, he had been through what I'd been through, he also had Hypothyroidism. He also explained to me that the years of stress and digestive issues were linked to this new diagnosis. He suspected I did in fact have the autoimmune disease, Hashimotos and he promised to test me for it. He explained that we had to work on my gut and my stress in order to heal the thyroid. He had a plan and it wasn't just medication. At that moment I knew I had to hold onto this guy. When he told me the program would cost about $3,000, even though I was making very little money as a twenty-two year old, recent college grad, I paid it on the spot. I was listening to my heart's desire to feel better and I just knew that this was the right path.

I'm pretty sure my parents and everyone else for that matter thought I was nuts. Back then, people didn't really know about functional medicine and holistic measures the way they do now. It didn't matter if other people didn't understand, I knew that I was on the right track. I knew so deeply in my being that this would be the thing to turn the tides.

At this point in my life I really needed support and guidance. Not just in my health but in my personal life. I was living with my first boyfriend, post college, in a small apartment in downtown NYC. I fell hard for him. I was swept off my feet with the flowers and the extravagant car and the way he built me up to be this *perfect* woman. I was so in love with this perfect guy…or so I thought.

After I moved in with him things began to change. It was so slow and insidious—I didn't even know what was happening until it was too late. He started pitting me against my family and my friends, making it so that his opinion and voice was the only one that mattered. He started calling me names, tearing me down, spying on all my conversations and hacking into my computer and phone. Gathering data that he would hoard and then use against me later. The grip was tightening but I didn't want to see the red flags, the warning signs. It got to a place where I was so low, so depressed, and stuck in fight or flight all the time. I started to cut myself as a way to release the pressure. I didn't have any other resources, I didn't know myself, I didn't have a guiding truth. It was a very low time in my life as I felt as though nothing I did was right and that I had to fit myself into a little tiny box the way he wanted me to be. In retrospect, knowing what I know about health now, it is no surprise that during this time of emotional trauma my autoimmune thyroid disease decided to rear its head. It was while I was dating him that all the symptoms started to appear that drove me to the initial doctor's visit.

We know Autoimmune Disease requires three things to manifest:

1. Genetics
2. A Trigger/Stressor
3. Leaky Gut

Well hot damn, I had stress in spades, day in and day out from the relationship plus trying to make it as a Broadway Stage Manager but being paid in subway cards and a lunch sandwich. Talk about high stress and pressure. I was just trying to be perfect in order to receive love. I figured if I could just people please I wouldn't upset anyone and therefore I was safe. I was essentially a walking ball of stress!

As far as leaky gut goes, well I learned pretty quickly from Dr. G that this was definitely occurring and probably had been happening without my knowledge for about seven years, ever since the IBS diagnosis. Leaky gut is when the tight junctions that line your small intestine open or are damaged from chemicals, toxins, inflammatory foods and stressors. When this happens for long periods of time, like in my case, it irritates the immune system, 70-80% of which lies beneath the surface of the lining of the small intestine. My immune system had been getting irritated for so long that it had started attacking its own tissue, my thyroid, causing antibodies and tissue destruction. My body was literally attacking me from the inside. Fun right?

So here I am, age twenty-three, feeling completely out of control in my personal life, professional life, and in my own body and then I meet a glimmer of hope and I fully jump in to repairing my health. What I didn't know was that this one decision to prioritize me, to put it all on faith, to jump fully in without knowing exactly what would happen, was the biggest catalyst for change in my life. It was my first leadership moment.

Within two weeks of being in his program my symptoms started to dissipate and by the end of the program I felt like a normal twenty-three year old again. My hair stopped falling out, the weight melted off, my energy came back, the brain fog and memory loss got better, the depression and anxiety lifted and my constant runs to the bathroom were a thing of the past. Then something funny happened, with this renewed control and strength in my health, I had a light bulb moment.

It was 5:30am and I was woken up from my deep sleep by my boyfriend (yet again) screaming at me and pacing in our tiny apartment. I sat up, blurry eyed and bewildered. He came into focus—looking at him I saw an angry, sad and bitter man. Someone who really had to figure out his own issues. I realized for the first time—this does not have to be my life, I don't deserve to be treated this way, I can have more and the only person keeping me here is me. I waited for a break in the yelling and I very calmly said, "I am moving out… today." He stopped dead in his tracks and said, "Well we had a good run", turned and walked out of the apartment and I never saw him again.

By the next day I was fully moved back into my parents home. Shaken up, full of fear but also full of, dare I say it, Freedom? Suddenly the fear was about, who am I? The emotions crashed over me like a 20' wave.

Who am I?

What do I like?

What do I think?

What do I want my life to be like?

If I could do anything, what would it be?

That's the thing about emotional and verbal abuse, you lose yourself. You lose your voice, your own opinions. So here came the real work. The work in finding myself.

Recovering my health gave me the strength to step fully into who I was meant to be, to stand up for myself, to demand more and better, to find my voice and later to be a voice for other women.

Flash forward a few years, fully empowered in my body, feeling incredible. I started a new career in events, realizing that theater was not something that was working for me any longer. It was 2016 and I was watching my client step onto stage representing Monsanto talking about how organic food wasn't any better for you and that we should eat conventional pesticide heavy foods. It was as if I could feel every organ exposed, the anger flooded every cell in my body. I knew I had to get out of that room. I ripped my headset off my head and told my boss I couldn't be there (a pretty bold move for a junior event planner), but I didn't care anymore. There was no way I could work another single second for someone who worked for a company that had been partially responsible for destroying my health.

I had just recovered from constant bloating, running to the bathroom after every meal; the crippling autoimmune disease of Hashimoto. A recovery process that had taken almost ten years, countless doctors, costly medical procedures, not to mention the multiple days taken from me getting to just be another kid. My teenage years were spent crumpled over, unable to move from the pain.

During my recovery process, I had learned from the functional medicine doctor that clean organic whole foods did wonders for my IBS and my thyroid. I knew exactly which foods actually worked and guess what? Pesticide ridden foods, wasn't it. And that's why I walked out of the room and never looked back.

Later that night I knew without a doubt that I needed to enroll to be a health coach because I could no longer empower someone like him. I wanted to be the VOICE empowering women with the knowledge of what to feed themselves to recover from chronic illness. I KNEW I HAD TO BE LOUDER THAN HIM so I enrolled in school that night! Whipped out a credit card and put it on faith! (Again!)

For the next year, I worked my 60+ hour work week in events and studied with the spare minutes I had. When I graduated, I quit my job, determined to 'help people'.

Ha! I can almost laugh at myself now, thinking back to this naive mid twenties version of me. Foraging forward with a good heart to help people but with zero business experience. Well, needless to say, this approach did not work. The first few years of the business were terrifying. It was like free falling without a safety net. I did odd jobs and worked as a contractor for my old company in order to pay the bills. I think one year I filed my taxes and I had about four different employers including my own company. Can you say hustle?

About two years into struggling to really launch my health coaching business I had reached my breaking point. I was running all over NYC, working crazier hours than I did as an event planner. I was so stressed out trying to survive that all my gut issues and anxiety came right back. Yep, all those issues I had spent so much time trying to reverse were worse than ever and here I was trying to be a coach that helped people with those very issues. It was a nightmare.

At that point I had an opportunity from the events company for a gig that would bring me about $15k over 3 months but it would mean sacrificing my business again to focus on the other work.

I had to ask myself, was I going to stay stuck and keep taking money from the events company? Or was I going to go all in on my business the same way I did on my health?

I had to become dependent on myself, no one was coming to save me. I had to make the decision to stop playing small, to release the fear and own my power as a coach. I had to become the leader of my life AGAIN. I had to become my own ATM.

I made the bold decision to decline the offer with the events company and instead elected to spend the time working on my limiting beliefs and building the business. There were a lot of dark nights of the soul, my shadow self came out telling me I couldn't do it and that I should give up, and there was more than one time that I thought about calling my old boss and getting my job back. But I stuck it out. I did the meditations, the affirmations, the journaling. I felt like one of those weirdo self help people and I'm pretty sure, yet again, everyone from my old life thought I had jumped off the deep end. But then a few months later, the magic happened. I had my first 15K MONTH helping women recover their hormones and gut! I remember being straight up flabbergasted looking at my bank account because I had never even seen that much money before.

From there the momentum has only grown. It's been 2 years since that first 15k month and I've helped over 200 women restore their health, reclaim their voice and live life on their terms. I have created a movement for women's health and I don't plan on stopping. I believe women are even more powerful than they know, that our hormones can be used as superpowers and that often the only thing holding us back in our health and our mindset. When we can overcome the limiting beliefs, use our feminine intuition, lead with our hearts, love ourselves deeply, declare what we want in life and heal from the inside out... *we are unstoppable.*

SOPHIE SHEPHERD

Sophie Shepherd is the founder of SHE Talks Health & the creator of the SHE Talks Health Podcast. Sophie is a Functional Health Coach focused on helping women understand the interconnection between their period, thyroid, gut and brain health and how to take an holistic approach to bringing their body back into balance. Her mission is to revolutionize the way women claim their health and slay old stories of being in sick bodies.

As a Functional Diagnostic Nutrition Practitioner and creator of SHE Thrives, Sophie helps educate and empower women around the globe to transform their hormones, brain and gut health through a combination of root cause diagnostic testing, nutrition & lifestyle science so they can finally have straightforward answers to their most mystifying symptoms and get their lives back!

Website: www.shetalkshealth.com

Instagram: @shetalkshealth

Facebook: SHE Talks Health

THE GATEWAY TO SELF-EMPOWERMENT

They say some are 'born leaders' and although leadership may come more naturally to some, I believe everyone has the potential and it's a choice to work towards it or not. It can look different for everyone too, some lead largely and loudly, others self-lead and others fall somewhere in between. Being a leader can be as simple as honoring your gifts and holding yourself accountable as you pursue your dreams. Yet, so often people get stuck due to their disempowered identity and limiting beliefs, which were created from their past experiences and ironically, are there to challenge them and help them grow as individuals. The beliefs can be released and replaced by empowering ones, and their identity is liquid and ever evolving as they grow and transform in their life journey.

This is a story of how I chose to reinvent myself in my early teenage years. When I chose to take my biggest fear and turned it into my biggest strength. I chose to release my old self perception and the belief that I was shy, and shifted it into feeling worthy of owning who I was while stepping into the light.

That was the beginning of my journey as a leader, which fueled my love for personal development and eventually made me a coach and leader in my industry. Simultaneously, as I write this I am three months postpartum, so I've had a whole new identity shift. It's interesting how the timing of writing this chapter shares parallels to what I'm experiencing now.

As a young girl I was far from the leadership type. I was extremely shy, like I couldn't speak to more than 3 people at once without having my heart pounding, hands sweating, body and voice trembling and words drifting off leaving me speechless kind-of-shy. All the while, deep down I yearned for the spotlight and influence I saw some of my peers had, because deep down I knew I was made for more than hiding behind my shyness.

Now as a coach having worked with clients of various professions and walks of life, I can say with certainty that this is a challenge that even outgoing people face. The fear of being seen fully; real, raw and vulnerable, and the fear of being judged, both block so many from embracing their unique gifts and personal potential, which often results in an unfulfilled life that is then filled with material stuff.

It is our preconceived notions, like our internal beliefs and our identity that cloud our light. Thoughts like, "I am not good enough" or "What will they think or say" or "I should do XYZ because it's what I'm supposed to do," stop us from showing up fully and authentically, which lowers our innate magnetism as a human. The magnetism that draws what we desire unto us.

Have you ever met someone that just pulls you in energetically? Like you can't help but want to listen, talk and befriend that person? The kind of person you want to keep around, because you sense a magic within them, and a way of being that you want to have too? That magnetism is within each of us, it's part of our potential and available when we choose to show up in our truth, leaning into what excites us and what feels aligned, no matter what the ego or others think. That magnetism is that kind of energy I yearned for as a young girl. I wanted to be that girl that people felt drawn to, the girl that wasn't afraid of trying new things, or of putting herself out there, being brave and bold.

When seventh grade ended my parents told us we were moving to the US, and I was ecstatic. I would get to go to a coed American school like in the movies, (when you live in a third world country as a young teenager, American movies are EVERYTHING) and most importantly I could start my social life from scratch.

Little thirteen year old Carla was determined to become outgoing and confident. She didn't know how, but she knew she had to, so she intuitively decided to begin acting like she was outgoing and confident, and it was through those actions that she proved to herself that she was.

On my first day of school I was both nervous and excited, I didn't know anyone, which was scary but also meant a clean slate. I walked into my first class, sat down and instantly mustered up the guts, against my own nature, to introduce myself to the girl sitting next to me. With hands sweating, and heart pounding, I turned around and said: "Hi my name's Carla, what's your name?" Seconds later it turned out she was also from Venezuela and we had identical class schedules. Now she's one of my best friends.

I kept doing this time and time again, getting uncomfortable, introducing myself and starting conversations with everyone I felt drawn to meet. And person by person, the once shy girl became outgoing, a master at small talk and confident in her own skin. Through my own actions I proved to myself that those preconceived notions were not mine to keep, and that I could release them and choose again. Through my actions, I proved to myself that I could become whoever I wanted to be.

Okay so I became Miss popular, cool. Except I knew I wasn't done. Ask me to speak in front of class and I would crumble. So I chose again, and volunteered to share my poem in front of the class. I was terrified. I raised my hand, which was shaking uncontrollably and that felt embarrassing enough, but I knew I had to do it. When the teacher asked me to take my turn, I stood up and began to read, while feeling my heart pound so hard it felt like it was going to come out of my chest. I must have read it so fast, that before I knew it, I was done, back on my chair, heart still pounding, sweat running down my face, feeling somewhat embarrassed and mostly proud. That day I proved to myself that I could do anything, and that was the beginning of me building my confidence to share my voice.

I kept putting myself out there, and every time it felt a little easier. Fast forward to now, and I'm a strong public speaker, and love using my words and energy to inspire and lead. Would I have stayed believing - "I'm shy and a bad public speaker" and "No one is interested in what I have to say" - I would have never had the guts to make outstanding (and funny!) wedding speeches, be the President of the American Marketing Association in College, teach yoga and breathwork classes, become the Assistant Director of a Summer Camp fresh out of college and later go on to speak at large leadership events and run leadership workshops.

All it took was choosing to change, to believe, think, feel, speak and act differently, and through it prove to myself that I could. Every action came from the new belief that I was a confident and magnetic public speaker. And although my previous beliefs challenged that through my nerves and lack of experience, I kept doing it over and over again until the old beliefs dissolved and the new ones prevailed.

Along my journey to become a strong public speaker and outgoing gal I became fascinated with personal development, which led me to become a Success Coach, Master NLP Practitioner and Hypnotherapist.

NLP (Neurolinguistic Programming) is a fancy word to describe how we use the basic language of our mind to consistently achieve the results we want in our life. It's like the instructions manual to our mind, and something I wish I had back in seventh grade. With it, I would have more easily upgraded my beliefs and felt more confident right off the bat, while taking action as my new outspoken and outgoing self.

From the moment we are conceived our Subconscious Mind begins taking inventory of our experiences and it gathers that information into groups that are similar. In other words, it generalizes and assumes certain things to fill in the gaps. For example: If I felt safe being quiet, then my mind generalized it and stored it as the internal decision: "If I stay quiet, I stay safe." That internal decision became a filter that influenced my identity and hence the way I thought, spoke, acted and felt. Can you think of certain experiences you had as a child that you can draw a connection to the way you are right now?

We can always disprove these internal decisions or beliefs and replace them with new ones. Through speaking up I created the new decision: "If I speak up, I share my truth and magnetize the people and the results I want."

Our actions are influenced by our internal beliefs, and powered by our emotions, and our emotions are charged by our past experiences. Every single emotional reaction that we have comes as a result of a collection of experiences, all of which we may or may not remember.

The best example of this in action is road rage. When someone cuts you off and you get angry, you're not necessarily angry at that person. Except when you were young you may have witnessed adults having road rage, which created the internal decision, "Get angry when someone cuts you off." Compound that with your own experiences on the road. Perhaps the first time someone cut you off you felt frustration, but you easily got over it. By the tenth time your frustration turns to anger, then someone cuts you off on a day you didn't sleep well and spilled coffee on your white shirt, so before you know it, you are cursing at the stranger who cut you off on their way to the hospital to have a baby. Your past experiences built on your frustration, charging the emotion of anger, so you lashed out unnecessarily. What's worse, now you're probably in a bad mood.

Our past experiences create our internal beliefs and charge our emotions, creating our internal programming and the lenses through which we experience our reality. Within that internal programming lives our identity, personal values and the potential we perceive ourselves to have, which affect our behavior and therefore our results.

The Subconscious Mind is the machine behind who we are. It not only runs our body and everything that happens behind the scenes that we don't think about, like breathing while we walk and talk, but it's also the key to embodying the best version of ourselves. You can be like me back in seventh grade and change who you perceive yourself to be through changing your actions, and through repetition, patience and perseverance make it happen; or you can change the subconscious programming and make that shift quicker and with more ease.

The Subconscious Mind processes 2 million bits per second of the information we are bombarded with daily and we consciously only handle 126 bits per second of that information. The lenses through which we see our reality are the filters that delete, distort and generalize the information, and what's left is what we can consciously process and comprehend within our unique reality. So you may take in a story one way and the person sitting next to you another way. This is why sometimes arguments go unresolved, and History is recounted in 100 different ways.

Every single person has a unique point of view or perception of the world, which projects onto their reality. To change the reality we must change the filters and to change the filters we must bypass the Subconscious Mind's bodyguard, the Critical Factor.

This 'bodyguard' sits between the Conscious and Subconscious Mind and guards the Subconscious Mind, so no unwanted information that is out of line with our filters can come through. That is why we see more of what we think and focus on. In other words, if you believe you aren't a creative person, no amount of training will make you creative. Just like if you don't believe it's possible for you to have financial freedom, then even if you all of the sudden make a ton of money, you will most likely end up spending it all and going back to living paycheck by paycheck. Our perception of the world blocks us from our own potential.

The Critical Factor or Subconscious Mind 'bodyguard' protects your view of the world, even if that view is not helping you grow, transform and get what you want in life. During our formative years, from conception until the age of seven, the Critical Factor is not fully formed, so we take everything at face value. If our parents or teachers acted a certain way, we took it as that's the way to be. For example: I was at the Chiropractor the other day and a toddler wanted to say hi to my baby daughter Camila, so I shared her name with the toddler. The dad responded for her by saying: "Sally, tell her you aren't good with names." Sally is taking that as a fact, and will most likely believe she's not good with names.

They say kids are sponges for a reason, those young years strengthen our internal filters, and begin to build our library of values and beliefs. Our experiences during those years may have been mostly out of our control, but once the Critical Factor is formed, we get to choose what we want our reality to look like through bypassing the bodyguard by entering into a light trance. I know this may sound unconventional but you are actually already doing it daily.

Marketers bypass everyone's bodyguard with commercials all the time. Have you ever tried talking to someone while they watch TV and it's like they can't hear you? That's because they are in a trance. We go in and out of trance throughout the day depending on what we are doing. Have you ever driven home and not remembered how you got there and whether you stopped at the red light or not? That's because you entered a light trance while you drove on autopilot. If you saw any billboards, chances are you took in the information at face value and it may affect your actions down the road. This might explain why you decided to buy a certain product out of nowhere.

When we go into a trance, we bypass the bodyguard and become more suggestible. Meaning we are more easily convinced, just like we did back in our formative years. And just like marketers can easily convince you to head out to the Apple store to get the newest iPhone, you can convince yourself that you are worthy and ready for your new upgraded beliefs. NLP uses different techniques with light trance to bypass the bodyguard and upgrade our beliefs and values so that the lenses of our reality align with our desired identity, goals and outcomes.

So whether you were a born leader or desire to be one, your Subconscious Mind holds the key to you being and achieving that which you desire. And whether you have a deep desire to lead yourself into your dream life or a group of people towards a common goal; you get to step into the best version of yourself through reprogramming your beliefs, values and identity. Every waking moment we get to choose who we are. We get to evolve and choose again, and again. Your power of choice is the gateway to your most empowered self, so you can magnetize the results and life you desire.

CARLA MARCONI

Carla Marconi is the Founder of Soul Rhythm Coaching, a podcast host and a Certified Master Practitioner of NLP, Hypnotherapist and Life Success Coach. She's a Prenatal Yoga Teacher, Meditation and Breathwork Facilitator. She helps new and expecting moms master the inner game of balancing being a mom and a professional, by upgrading their belief systems and empowering them with strategies to never lose themselves within motherhood, so they can feel confident inside and outside the home. Carla uses her unique blend of breathwork and hypnotherapy to help her clients feel calm, grounded, confident and in charge. Carla has 4 years of coaching experience supporting mom entrepreneurs and since entering motherhood herself she's gained a new understanding of what it takes to run a business and a home. Carla was raised in Venezuela and lives in Tampa, FL with her husband Bryan, daughter Camila and golden doodle Swayze.

Website: www.soulrhythmco.com

Instagram: @carla.soulrhythm

EMPOWER THE EMBER & HONOR THE HUMAN

She knew she could do it. Hesitant, nervous, she peeked out from the shadows deep down within me, but she knew she could do it. She knew she had an incredibly, brilliantly, strong and powerful force that could face any fear head on. After all, it was she who had held and supported my mom with unconditional love and empathy through the last few years of her life before she passed away. There is a certain type of leadership and strength that emerges when one is asked to witness and guide the slow, long drawn out passing of a mother in hospice—especially when your mom understands you better than anyone else in the world.

Let me introduce you to She. *She* is my Higher Self.

My Higher Self had been suppressed for many years, through societal expectations, family challenges, and unhealthy relationships. I kept her dormant, hidden. However, I felt her from time to time as a rumbling ember, a powerful spark, whenever I'd feel rage creep in or a boundary about to be crossed. But on this average Wednesday on the fourteenth floor of a tall Chicago office building, I kept her hidden and quiet. All the while secretly hoping she'd be noticed and encouraged to come to life, asked to emerge. I was afraid of what would happen if I let her loose. So, in this case, I kept her suppressed and instead of seeing her power, my project manager noticed the opposite, my ego—the fear, nerves, uncertainty. It felt like she had pushed my Higher Self back down further where I'd keep her hidden for several more years to come.

It was a pivotal project and moment in my career. It was the opportunity to present to and facilitate a workshop for thirty global C-Suite executives all on my own. This wasn't just any project. This project was redesigning a product for people with the same disease my mom passed away from. To inform the design of a product my mom used for seven years of her life. I'd get to be a catalyst to innovate on this product that my mom was forced to use for her condition and yet stripped her of her dignity every time she used it. It was a dream project. And to facilitate a design workshop for the project of my dreams to help people with the same condition as my mom—was the opportunity of a lifetime. This workshop would be the final step in a global research study I had just led, managed, and facilitated on my own.

Deep down I truly believed my Higher Self could emerge from the depths of me and nail that presentation. Ace it. But, she needed a leader to believe in her because I didn't fully trust myself yet. I needed a leader to believe in me and see my fullest potential—my Higher Self—along with my strengths, desire for success, and deep passion for this project that could impact millions of people with similar challenges as my mom had. What I really wanted was my project manager to ask me to step up into my bravery. To encourage me and help me to tap into and connect to my Higher Self, but instead my manager fed and leveraged the fear, nerves and uncertainty that had started to eat at my psyche and she said, "You can't present in front of the C-Suite executives because you'll get too nervous and mess up, so I'll do it myself."…My heart sank. Once again my Higher Self had been pushed down, ignored, oppressed, asked to hide, and this time she wasn't sure when she'd have any courage to show up again.

EMPOWER THE EMBER & HONOR THE HUMAN

A Forbes article called *With No Power Comes No Responsibility: How A Broken Corporate Culture Disempowers Employees* by Michael Solomon states, "When you disempower employees, you disregard and cast aside their humanity."

For me, it felt like my humanness (the fear, uncertainty, and nerves) were shamed instead of acknowledged and held. I wanted my project manager to ask my Higher Self to come out from hiding, to help me step into my own power—I wanted her to say to me that I *could* do it and that she'd be there to lead me, support me, encourage me. But instead it felt like she took any ounce of power and confidence I had and diminished it. I like to think she didn't mean to disempower me, she just truly wanted what was best for the project. Although, researchers on the topic of micromanagement and top-down control state that this is where the disconnect happens between the employees' desires, goals and aspirations, and the company's objectives.

As a leader myself, I've learned from this experience and now recognize that it's the leader's responsibility to connect with the team members and ask them questions about their aspirations and desires. Do they want to take the lead on this task, or do they genuinely need more support before they're on their own? What has their past experiences and successes or failures shown? Because come on, what's the worst that could've happened? I got a dry mouth or messed up a few times—but what if she asked me to envision the best thing that could happen? What if she had spent the time telling me I wouldn't be able to do it, and instead, had practiced the presentation with me so thoroughly that there was no way I'd mess up. It seems to be there was a need to control the situation on her part, vs. let me lead. I appreciate how this Forbes article called *Leaders Can Cultivate True Employee Empowerment*, by Murielle Tiambo articulates it:

> "Leaders can shy away from empowering their people if a fear of letting go and reluctance to deal with the unknown should crop up. Leaders need to then ask themselves: What is the likely outcome? What's the worst that can happen

if they make a mistake? What is the best that can happen if I let go and they succeed? What additional support can I offer?"

The question I ponder is, would I have succeeded if I had had more encouragement? I truly believe so. Especially if we had looked back at my previous success of facilitating several other smaller workshops on my own. I had successfully completed an entire 24-person research study, won an international design award in school a few years prior, and had interviewed for this very job the day my mother died—and nailed it.

Every person, team member, employee, new and old has an ember within them, a Higher Self that is begging to be recognized. We as leaders need to empower that power, and surrender our own egos and worries and believe in these future leaders. The first step is to look at ourselves and ask, are we trying to control this situation? Why? And then ask the team member empowering questions and gather enough information to assess their level of comfort and desire paired with the riskiness of the project and task at hand. Their inner ember wants to be seen, strengthened, and encouraged just like we do. Can we let go and trust another's ember? Another's Higher Self? What's holding us back?

* * *

ONE WEEKEND SPENT IN A SMALL, hidden, historic building in London in mid-August was all it took. I spent two long days in a transformational program and by Sunday night, for the first time, I met the "thoughts in my head," and discovered a brand new way of seeing the world. It just took two days for me to learn one of the most important lessons I'll ever learn: my emotions and past trauma are my responsibility—no one else's. Not my mom's, dad's, sisters' manager's, friends', or boyfriend's. Mine. That weekend softened me. It slowly broke down a wall I had around my heart I didn't know existed.

The Friday before the program I got into an argument with my manager (who my entire team found challenging to work with). By Monday I had apologized and took responsibility for my defensiveness, she had apologized back, and at the end of the meeting we cried together about our past hurt in the workplace, and why we had argued.

From then on she became my biggest advocate. She had seen my Higher Self and befriended her. From then on emotional intelligence and raising consciousness became one of my top values. This short but impactful experience taught me the power and importance of emotional intelligence and higher consciousness in leadership in the workplace—without my ability to see the situation from a broader view (higher consciousness), and take responsibility for my side of the street (emotional intelligence), we would have stayed in the same unconscious loop only making the other person wrong and never building a positive relationship. Never seeing each other for the humans that we are, nor honoring each other's Higher Selves.

I had only just started my career, but I was in for a rude awakening that most leaders in the business world had not discovered the importance of, nor explored their own emotional intelligence or consciousness, let alone tapped into their Higher Selves.

Fast forward to a few years later where I landed a new job with new leaders. The office door creaked open and my body immediately went into flight or fight response. This was a daily occurrence at another big corporate company, and this was the door of the executive director of our team. She was one of the most intimidating women I had ever met. She scared me. She was several years older than me and had this incredible confidence and self-sureness that I had never seen before. But this also meant you didn't want to get on her 'bad side.' She was the opposite of approachable.

Because of the inner healing work I had done (and was doing) on myself, and because at this point connected to my Higher Self regularly, I knew that my trigger response to her opening her office door was because of my own past trauma. Still, I was triggered each time because I didn't like how she treated me and my colleagues. The way this woman treated others and led her team was nothing like I'd seen before. I observed her in every meeting, watched how she interacted with her direct reports, and even kept an eye on her extensive email behavior on vacation. I was in awe. It seemed she had little compassion for her teams' humanness and her own.

She exuded a harshness, judgment, and a strict edge. I watched her expect the world from her team to no end. I was sometimes the target of her reactionary emails. Still, as someone who had always wanted to learn from and connect to higher profile, older female leaders, I was disappointed she wasn't the female leader I had dreamed of learning from. After a year on the job I realized my lesson wasn't to learn from her how to lead, but in fact it was to learn how *not* to lead. The lesson was also to tap into my Higher Self and my now matured emotional intelligence and higher consciousness on this very experience with her. It was to practice compassion and acknowledge her humanness, even though I so desperately wanted *her, my leader*, to teach me these things, and act this way towards me. Well, she did teach me, just not in the way I had expected.

I started to realize I'd need to step into my own power, and deeply connect to my Higher Self if I wanted to see any change. This experience with her required me to step into my own conscious, heart-centered, emotionally intelligent leadership. I took it as an opportunity. I started to ask her all the right questions in every meeting to ensure she knew she was heard and understood. I identified her triggers and (without her knowing), spoke to those parts of them that were fearful, uncertain, and had a hard time trusting or letting go of control. I made sure to be overly communicative to support her in her role, and I found parts of her to genuinely compliment and appreciate.

After a while, I started to heal that scared part of me. I wasn't triggered so much when she'd open the door. I started to not take her reactions and behavior personally and soon I was able to have compassion for the scared little girl inside her, only trying to be liked, to be successful, and only put on a harsh facade to survive and stay safe. I had compassion for the fact that her own Higher Self had lost her way.

A few years and one pandemic later, I spent a few months at a small business in a director level position. Since I had several years of corporate experience under my belt, and truly understood what to look for in a company, I was vocal from the beginning that what I looked for in a company was strong emotional intelligence and clear conscious communication. The whole team agreed they did as well, and after a few months I experienced that most of them practiced what they preached. However, one colleague shared with me how she also valued emotional intelligence, yet I started to notice a different story.

The most challenging experiences I came across in this role were with this woman. Interestingly enough she was younger than me, yet just as intimidating and scary as the previous executive director I had worked with. She also exuded a harshness, judgment, and a strict edge. There were several moments I witnessed her lightness, her friendly side, her loving heart, but it seemed to me she believed that to be compassionate or patient with herself or others, she'd need to sacrifice working hard. Over the few months I worked with this team she'd have several incredibly intense emotional reactions towards me (and others), and exuded blame, unkind words and a harshness. In most trigger scenarios such as this, I believe there are usually two sides to the story, and in most cases both sides could have done something differently to have made the experience go more smoothly.

Then, I got the chance to truly practice. One day she sent me several reactionary messages about a particular project deliverable. It took me a few hours to move through my own trigger (which I acknowledge as caused by my own trauma), within me. I took a few deep breaths, acknowledged my own pain and re-read the messages with a newfound perspective that she wasn't intending to blame me or cause harm. She clearly had her own challenges and traumas that I had triggered and she wanted what was best for the project. I saw her as human. As someone who had been hurt and disappointed by others in the past. She needed to fight for herself, and in this case fighting meant abruptly and harshly messaging me. I sent a calm message back and delivered the items she requested all on time.

I took a step back. I saw that her words towards me were less about *me* and the situation, and more about her overall view of the world. People disappoint her. No one cares about her. She's not heard. I wanted to see if we could heal our past trauma wounds together, through this experience. I honestly wanted to be the person who could inspire her to rewrite this story. I saw her potential, her loving heart, and her eagerness to succeed and be liked.

So, the following week we sat down for a follow up and the first thing she did was apologize. I took it upon myself to step into my leadership and didn't argue, get defensive, or shame her. Instead I thanked her. I thanked her for her apology and told her I accepted it. I asked if I could share my side of the experience, and she listened. She shared her side. I listened. We asked how we could do better next time. She even took notes. I could see she was eager to change. I then vulnerably shared about my past trauma and why it was so triggering for her to send me such harsh messages. She listened with a sense of sorrow and empathy listening to my experiences as a sensitive introverted soul. She then opened up and shared her past trauma as to why she reacts this way. I listened with my heart wide open and empathized, and started to understand our differences. We decided on a few solutions of how to best communicate moving forward and I felt a shift in our relationship.

To this day I am grateful for these women. They allowed me to learn more about myself and my capacity to lead, to inspire compassion for someone who doesn't have compassion for themselves, and gave me a chance to grow my leadership skills. I realize now there are some leaders that aren't meant to become a heart-centered leader as I envision it. Perhaps a heart-centered leader is also someone who inspires us to dive deeper into our own hearts, and perhaps helps us bring more softness and compassion to the world.

John Mackey, (CEO of Whole Foods) speaks to compassion in his inspirational book, Conscious Leadership, *"...compassion arise[s] out of recognition of our shared suffering and pain. In light of the reality of suffering, isn't it the single best response we can have toward ever living, being compassion? Leaders who feel and express authentic compassion awaken a deep spiritual quality within their inner selves that will inspire other people. True compassion creates trust, commitment, and loyalty in others. Compassion brings us together and reminds us what is most important in life."*

I've come to understand that projects, workshops, meetings, deliverables, while important in their own way, are minuscule compared to the importance of our humanness. I believe we need to put our team members' humanity first, above all else, empower the ember, and evoke the Higher Self within.

HANNAH IRENE DUFFY

Hannah is a designer, visionary, and healer—her corporate career spans 10+ years working as a design researcher and innovation consultant, and her healing career spans 7+ years studying and coaching within self-development and spirituality. Her purpose in life is to infuse her passion for her own spiritual growth and self-development to help solve the challenges our world and current leaders face, particularly within the areas of anti-hunger/food security, nutrition, climate consciousness, and conscious leadership. As a certified Kundalini Yoga teacher, her daily sadhana practice has supported her to step into her own power to create change in this world and lead with consciousness and love. She hopes her chapter inspires, empowers, moves, and excites you, reminds you to be gentle with yourself and your own humanness, and encourages you to offer even an ounce more of compassion to yourself and others.

Instagram: @hanbans193

Facebook: facebook.com/hduffy2

LinkedIn: linkedin.com/in/hduffy/

TURNING ASHES TO GOLD—A PATH TO LIBERATION & LEADERSHIP THROUGH THE BODY

PART ONE: FIRED

There I was standing at the check-in counter in the Atlanta Airport, being asked to remove weight from the extremely massive bag I was wanting to check. It was 6am and my eyes were still swollen from the tears I cried the night before. My face was puffy and I was trying desperately to keep down the nausea that came with being five weeks pregnant.

As I frantically removed random objects from my bag into the trash to avoid the $100 fee, I could feel the tears beginning to stream down my face. I kept telling myself, "Lauren, just hold it together you're almost home. Not here. Not now."

Boarding the plane, I couldn't help but wonder if the flight attendants working my flight back home to Denver knew that I had just been fired from training to do exactly what they were doing now. I wondered if they had a note on their tablet stating "Lauren Valdes, fired from Flight Attendant school." Maybe more-so, fired for being a "bully"…a "mean girl".

On my three hour flight back to Denver, I kept fighting back the tears. I shifted between feeling deep levels of shame and grief in my body, to trying to not puke right there on the plane.

It felt as though I was on a flimsy raft, riding between the waves of feeling everything to feeling absolutely nothing. And honestly, that's all I wanted at that point, was to be so numb that I wouldn't have to face or deal with any of it.

I wouldn't have to face Justin, my partner of almost a decade, and tell him what had happened.

I wouldn't have to deal with the fact that I had a baby growing in my womb, and that in nine months I would be a mother—*my absolute biggest fear*.

I wouldn't have to feel the rejection, the heartbreak, the pure disbelief that I had just been fired.

Me, Lauren Megan Valdes ... *FIRED*!!

PART TWO: INVITATION INTO THE BODY

Let's take it back for a moment shall we? I'm sure you're wondering how I ended up here. On a plane, pregnant and fired from flight attendant school.

Before we get into all of that, I want to invite you in for a moment to breathe and connect into the body. Placing one or both hands somewhere on the body. Creating a sense of connection, a sense of presence and aliveness.

I'll share more on this in a bit, but the seemingly simple act of connecting to the body is what pulled me out of a space of feeling completely hopeless, lost and disconnected to where I am now—the creator of a successful online coaching company and brand, mother to the most joyful daughter, partner to the love of my life, 'Pleasure Priestess', and the go to somatic trauma healer for women desiring to feel empowered enough to create lives, businesses and relationships filled with pleasure and sacred purpose.

It's what gave me the courage, strength and divine power to start again. To birth my baby out of hospital, without medication and limited intervention. To begin a business supporting and empowering women to step boldly into their feminine expression. And to leave my ten year relationship, find pleasure and intimacy with myself and fall back in love with the same man eleven months later.

This is what allowed me to soften, open, surrender and trust that everything happened for a reason. And that me being fired from flight attendant school and being pregnant with my daughter was in fact the most needed redirection of my life.

While you read my chapter and perhaps you can pull this into other chapters, I invite you to slow down, to breathe deeply in through the nose and out through your mouth. To allow your jaw to unhinge, your pelvic bowl to unclench and your heart to open.

Allow your breath to become soft, opening yourself up to possibility.

In through the nose and out through the mouth.

Pulling the breath from the roots of the body, from the roots of the Divine Mother into your heart. And letting the cosmic flow of the Divine Masculine penetrate your crown and fill your body with light.

Letting the synergy of both energies hold you. Letting yourself be seen and supported.

Letting yourself fully unravel.

Beautiful, my love. You have arrived. No matter where you are on your journey....

YOU. HAVE. ARRIVED.

I wish so badly someone would have whispered those words to me, when I needed them most.

I wish someone would have told me, "Lauren this is it. This is your moment."

PART THREE: THE MEDICINE

In reality, I applied to be a flight attendant out of pure desperation for purpose and a sense of belonging.

I was living in Denver with my partner, Justin, nannying and feeling pretty lost in life.

I found myself in Network Marketing, praying it would be my out...my way to freedom.

My upline, I had known from Tampa (my hometown) and she had just gotten a job as a flight attendant for one of the top US carriers.

I remember seeing her posts on Facebook and thinking it was the most glamorous job—travel the world and run my "business". Sounds like a dream, right?

So I went through the application process and applied at a few different companies. I ended up getting an offer with a backup company and I had it set in my mind that that was where I would undergo training and begin my oh so glamorous career.

Two weeks before I was supposed to leave for training with that company, I received a call from Atlanta and was offered a position with my "dream" company. I was elated.

Truly, I remember hopping off the phone with the sweet lady and her Southern accent and calling everyone and anyone that would answer.

The next day, I declined the first offer and began to prepare to be in Atlanta for eight weeks of training.

My world felt so filled with potential at that time. I mean this had to be it, I remember recording all the angel number sightings that obviously meant I was in pure alignment with my path and vision, right?

Two nights before I left for training, Justin was helping me pack and prep. It was a full moon and we were trying to spend as much time together as possible. It would be the longest stretch we had been apart from one another in eight years.

We made love that night and both of us knew that we were playing with fire choosing not to get Plan B.

It's a bit serendipitous to look back at this time, because I think we both knew unconsciously what we were choosing at that moment. Despite how terrified and set in not having children we were, I think unconsciously we knew that co-creating a baby and birthing a child into the world was exactly what both of us needed.

I ended up missing my period two weeks into training.

And as life would have it, God/Source/the Divine Creator gave us the exact medicine we needed.

PART FOUR: THE WOUNDED FEMININE

The wounded feminine will see other women as competition. She will use her voice and misdirected power to pull other women down, especially those who she views as a threat. Those who feel as though they are taking the attention off of her.

The wounded feminine will bash, hate and exile other women to make herself seem stronger, more worthy and more confident.

It's all for show though because at the end of the day, the wounded feminine is crying out for someone to validate her and make her feel worthy and enough.

She desires to be loved, adored and admired. She desires connection and safety. She desires to know what it feels like to put her guard down, to let herself be wild, free and completely unleashed.

Flight attendant training was maybe my first initiation into healing the wounded feminine and becoming more of the sacred feminine I embody now.

My sisterhood wound was laid out on the table during my month-long stretch of training.

I knew the moment I met my roommate, Amanda, that something felt off.

Our energies didn't match and without going into too much detail who I was and who she was were two completely different ends of the spectrum.

I remember feeling somewhat nervous going into training. I was never a girls-girls. I mean I had a handful of good girlfriends but I just remember always feeling like a bit of an outsider in female friendship groups.

And at the same time, I had made a commitment to myself to be open to every and all friendships while being in training. All I desired was to get through training, pass the rigorous tests and long hours and still be able to maintain my health and well-being.

I'm a down to Earth gal, super chill and honestly at the time, I was a bit of a stoner.

Without going into the nitty gritty, he-said-she-said details, I'll do my best to explain what happened.

From what I heard, Amanda felt pretty threatened by me after the first week of school. She had found herself a really beautiful network of close girlfriends and because I didn't yet feel completely safe in female friend groups, I found myself getting pretty close to three gay males.

We worked out together, went out together, studied together, walked to class together and spent a lot of time laughing with one another.

We literally had the best time and spent just about every waking hour with one another.

Our intention was never to exclude anyone, but apparently that is how Amanda and a few other girls in the class had felt.

Amanda was struggling to keep up in training.

After she failed one of the practicums, she was asked to explain what was attributing to her struggle and blamed me and my three friends for her inability to keep up in the very fast paced, hands-on learning environment.

There were five of us called in for disciplinary violations after training one day. I was the last to be talked to. It was about 11:30pm and being newly pregnant and not haven eaten in several hours, my brain could not comprehend what was happening.

All I remember was two women reading off what seemed like a pretty long list of adjectives to describe me and my behavior in training: "mean girl", "ring leader", "rude", "dismissive".

In a moment of complete disarray and complete emotional, mental and physical exhaustion I told them I thought I was pregnant, but was waiting for my boyfriend to come into town that weekend to take an official test.

I tried to explain that I didn't feel like my normal self and perhaps it was due to early pregnancy.

One of the women looked me dead in the eye and said very matter of factly that "I was not acting pregnant".

I shut down. I didn't have the brain power or the strength to fight the accusations.

I hadn't yet delved into the world of inner child healing, but looking back my little girl felt so unseen, so small, so misunderstood. It felt like I was back in Catholic School sitting in the principal's office.

The conversation ended with me feeling completely helpless and not knowing if I would be allowed to continue training. I was told that a decision would be made in a few days.

Justin came to Atlanta a few days later and in a very small hotel room of a Red Roof Inn, it was confirmed I was pregnant.

For a week, I could feel my body caving in. We were finally called back on the day of midterms and were asked to dismiss ourselves from training with flights booked for each of us to fly back home.

I called my parents the moment I got to my hotel room, hysterically mumbling out that not only had I been fired, but that I was pregnant.

They were more ecstatic about being grandparents than anything.

I feared so deeply seeing Justin. I knew how disappointed he was in me. I felt like a complete failure.

I mean I was, wasn't I?

For the next few weeks, I laid on the couch of our apartment attempting to keep my morning sickness at bay, binge watching *The Office* and *Friends* for the 100th time each, and unraveling the layers of shame I felt.

Finally, I cracked open the book 'The Universe Has Your Back' by Gabby Bernstein and saw it as a piece of divine intervention.

There it was. Confirmation before belief that there was a bigger plan to all of this. And that this in fact was a redirection. Through turmoil, I was given an opportunity to turn ashes into gold.

So I decided we would move back to Florida, I would become a mom, I would birth a baby unmedicated and out of hospital and start some sort of online coaching company.

PART FIVE: HEART-CENTERED LEADERSHIP

Leadership isn't something you get taught, especially heart-centered leadership.

It's something we have to learn. It's something we have to create for ourselves. And for many of us, we don't activate it fully in moments of perfection or bliss.

It's created in the moments where life feels hard, unbearable. In the moments where it feels like we're swimming up-stream through a current that won't ease up.

When we moved back to Florida, I found myself pregnant in my parent's house living in my childhood bedroom.

My vision was distorted, blurred at best. Yet, something in me knew I was meant to impact the world in really big ways.

At the time, I didn't realize that it was intuitive and would translate to teaching women pleasure and learning to facilitate somatic healing. I didn't even know what somatic healing was. I was so disconnected with my body at the time, that I didn't even know self-pleasure or intimacy outside of just "getting off".

What I did know was that my whole life was this big spiritual journey. I was raised Catholic and found myself a lot in bookstores often browsing the spirituality and personal development section.

Every turn within my life, felt as though I was being guided by something bigger than me. Something I couldn't grasp, but something I could unmistakably feel.

Becoming a mother gave me purpose in a new way and I realized that life was no longer about me. And, also I refused to sacrifice myself, my dreams and my desires.

So I journeyed the path of learning how to cultivate it all—to hold it all.

To be of service and to let my desires lead.

To be turned on and to hold myself in my own power.

To walk into a room with confidence and see the beauty in every single person.

And to be a leader, not by force, not by manipulation, but through love, compassion and unwavering conviction in who I am and what I stand for.

That to me is heart-led leadership. The anchoring into the knowing that all of this actually has nothing to do with you and at the same time, it has everything to do with you.

PART SIX: THE BODY IN EXPRESSION

I learned leadership through the expression of my body.

Somatic healing is just that, it's our ability and willingness to explore the seen and unseen elements that make us whole. To explore the pieces that have been layered by society, our family lineage and our own experience and to bring a sense of safety into all of it.

That's what changed everything for me.

My journey didn't get easier after I birthed my daughter, Elliott. It was actually the exact opposite, I was ripped wide open in so many ways.

I've had many moments curled up in a ball in the bathroom, holding myself and repeating "I am safe" over and over again until I embodied it.

I have also found radical self-love, liberation, abundance and pleasure in ways I never thought possible.

Connecting to my body and letting her express in the most raw ways, created space for me to receive more of what I actually desired in my life.

Heart-centered leaders don't hide from moments or truths that feel uncomfortable, they open themselves up fully in those experiences with a knowing that through the threshold, stepping boldly on the other side is pure bliss, remarkable expansion and the most holy surrender.

Before we end here, I want to invite you again to take a moment to place one hand or both on the body, breathing deeply and ask:

What do you desire from me?

What are you wanting to birth through me?

How are you desiring to be seen as a leader?

Show me my next steps...

And take a moment to pause, to listen, to tune in. The answers might come instantly through pulsations, sensations or a simple knowing or the answers may trickle in over the next few days, weeks and months.

Trust whatever comes alive within you.

Trust with unwavering doubt.

And know that whatever you are desiring is for you.

With so much love and gratitude.

Lauren

LAUREN MEGAN VALDES

Lauren Megan Valdes is a mother, somatic trauma healer, pleasure coach and priestess. Lauren heals and initiates women into the full spectrum divine feminine by connecting them back to their roots, womb and heart. Her mission is to help women heal, unravel and decondition from the beliefs and generational traumas that keep them from leading with desire, expressing their wild feminine and receiving the wealth, legacy and intimacy they crave.

Lauren currently lives in Tampa, FL with her daughter, Elliott, and partner of over a decade, Justin. When she isn't working with clients and expanding her mission, she is fully present in play and joy with her family.

Website: www.laurenmegan.com

Instagram: @the.pleasure.priestess

YOUR INNER NATURE LEADS THE WAY

You can only lead others as well as you are able to lead yourself. Your internal state will dictate the way you move through this external world. As a woman or a person with a womb, you have an inner blueprint that can give you hints as to how you can become more aligned with yourself in your personal and business life. It's called your menstrual cycle. It is my mission to help you become empowered through your menstrual cycle instead of feeling weighed down by it.

Important reminder: your menstrual cycle isn't your period. It is your 23-35 day cycle of hormonal fluctuations that your body goes through each month, with your period being just one phase out of four. The fluctuations you experience with your hormones each month impact your emotional, physical, and mental states. Becoming familiar with your cycle and your inner rhythms that you have each month will allow you to know when is the best time to create, take a break, use your voice and speak up, launch, rebrand, meet with potential clients, up your marketing, take time for solitude, and when it's time to show up for others.

This is something that I wish I knew as a young teenager. Instead, I grew up with painful periods, PMS, and a deep resentment for being a woman.

"Why couldn't I have just been born a man? Men have it way better."

"Being a woman sucks and I'm over it."

These thoughts frequented my mind often. Visits to my gynecologist didn't make it any better when all I was told was to get on birth control and that "it's just part of being a woman." So I got on birth control because if that was going to make my periods less painful, I was game. I grew up a sick child with asthma, digestive issues, food sensitivities, a weak immune system and depression that developed in my younger teenage years so I did what I thought could at least help one issue.

What I didn't know at the time was that hormonal birth control was about to make me feel worse and throw me into a deeper pit of feeling ill than I already did.

When I finally decided that I no longer wanted to put unnatural substances in my body and decided to embark on a pathway of holistically healing my body, I came to learn about how hormonal birth control completely cuts off the communication between your brain and your uterus. It also stops you from having a menstrual cycle. To me, this doesn't sound like things that should be interfered with. While this chapter isn't about birth control and my opinion on it, it is to shed light on very important information that Western medicine has failed to disclose with us as young teens/adults trying to navigate our menstrual cycles and period issues.

What does any of this have to do with leadership? It goes back to the very first line of this chapter that emphasizes being your own leader so that you can lead others. I had to go against what the Western medical system was telling me so that I could actually heal. It meant that I had to first be my own leader. It was up to me to do the work to educate myself on why my period was so painful and why having a menstrual cycle is important. It led me to unpacking a concept I didn't know existed.

This concept is called menstrual cycle awareness. It is the practice of living in alignment with your natural fluctuations and learning to work with the changes of your cycle instead of against them. This is important because certain phases of your cycle will require something different from you.

We are not linear beings, we are cyclical just like the Earth cycles through seasons. The problem is that we live in a masculine dominated society that has made us believe that we are meant to operate within the same structured way everyday. How can we possibly operate the same way everyday when we don't even *feel* the same everyday? We have hormonal fluctuations *every few days* that impact our emotions, our mental clarity, and how energized and social we feel.

This isn't to bash men or those without wombs, but to instead bring awareness to the fact that our physiology functions differently and therefore should be taken into consideration. Biological males operate with the cycle of the sun. This means that they operate on a 24 hour hormonal cycle like the sun that rises and sets the same each day. Biological women on the other hand align with the cycle of the moon, hence why sometimes people refer to having their period as "being on their moon time." There are 13 moon cycles in a year, women have on average 13 menstrual cycles each year, and since the moon operates on a 28 day cycle, it is never quite the same each day. There is a reason why the sun is associated with stable energy and the moon with changing emotions. In fact, the word "lunatic" comes from the latin word for moon, "luna" because of the connection that the phases of the moon can have on how we feel. Menstrual cycle awareness is the reminder that *feeling* isn't negative and that our emotions are messages from our body.

Each phase of the menstrual cycle is correlated with a season, elements, and a moon phase. To understand this further we must break the menstrual cycle down and get to know each of the four phases.

PHASE 1 - *MENSTRUATION*

Inner Season: *Winter*

Moon Phase: *New Moon*

Elements: *Air & Ether*

This is the first phase of your menstrual cycle, your period. During this phase the body is shedding the lining, blood, and mucus of the uterus since no fertilization of an egg has occurred. Your menstruation phase lasts for 3-7 days on average.

Your period is your Inner Winter season. On Earth during winter we see it is cold, dark, the leaves have fallen from the trees, some animals go into hibernation, and the flowers that were once blossoms have withered away. If you live in an area where you experience winter, you may be more inclined to eat warming foods like soups and roasted vegetables, stay indoors, rest, keep cozy, and wear proper clothes to keep you warm.

Similarly when you are in your inner winter, your bleeding time, it is a moment of slowing down, reflection, and rest. Heat means good blood circulation so it's essential to eat warming foods, teas, and take time to sit with how you're feeling.

The new moon within this phase also reflects this dark time where we embrace the things that need to die within our lives. When I talk about death in this chapter I don't mean human death, but instead the things that need to be let go of mentally, emotionally, & physically (your uterine lining). The new moon teaches us that death creates more space for the things that we want alive and thriving. So look at your period as the release to help you create more space in your life, in whichever way that applies to you.

The elements of air and ether represent the unseen forces that we can't see but can feel. Regardless of whatever religion, or spiritual practice you follow, air and ether are the elements that connect us to the spirit of our creator. So whatever or whoever you believe to be the almighty creator of your world, these elements connect you to that. There is no coincidence that we feel the most sensitive during this time because our intuition is the strongest.

When it comes to running a business this is not the time to pressure yourself to finish your to-do list. See where you can shorten your list or take a temporary break from it. Are you able to keep your business tasks as minimal as you can and to ones that don't take a lot of energy? This isn't the best time to force yourself to socially interact, finish a project, or to launch something new because your body is already going through such an energy draining process. It is okay to take a break from creating, working super hard, and being a social butterfly for just a few days.

This is however a great time to brainstorm what creativity seeds you wish to plant in the coming season. Make a list or spreadsheet of any ideas that come up during this time without the pressure of figuring out the final details of it yet. Write it out and come back to it after your period when your brain is more clear. Giving yourself this time to slow down will better help you show up for yourself so that you may show up for others.

PHASE 2 - *FOLLICULAR*

Inner Season: *Spring*

Moon Phase: *Waxing Moon*

Elements: *Water & Earth*

If when your period ends, you start to feel more energized, social, and overall just damn good, it's because you are entering the season of your Inner Spring. Is it a coincidence that seeds need Earth (soil) and water to help them sprout and grow? Hence why water and Earth are the two elements present during this time.

Your Follicular phase actually begins at the same time your period does but then continues thereafter for another 10-11 days on average. To keep it simple, this is a time when your brain communicates to your ovaries to start producing follicles. These follicles are sacs that will contain one immature egg in each. The healthiest egg will eventually mature and the other follicles will reabsorb back into the ovaries. In this case, the follicles are literally sprouting seeds, which are your eggs. Do you see the correlation already with the season of Spring? When you look at the nature around you, you will see bees pollinating, seeds sprouting, more animal activity, and things starting to warm up.

The moon is also waxing and getting closer to becoming full which is associated with a rise in your energy as well. This is an incredible time to focus on sowing the seeds of what you wish to create, nourishing the environment for them to sprout, and taking care of the sprouts so that they may grow into strong plants. Things to focus on during this time are starting projects, building new habits, and being more active. This season is a great time to launch in your business, do a workshop/live talk, record podcasts, videos, content, and get the more time consuming things done. It's normal to suddenly feel flooded with ideas. Enjoy this sense of renewal and use it to your advantage while you're there!

PHASE 3: *OVULATORY*

Inner Season: *Summer*

Moon Phase: *Full Moon*

Elements: *Fire*

You are in your prime during this time! This is the peak of your cycle where your energy is the highest, your creativity is peaking, and your sexual energy is exploding! You are the most magnetic at this point. Ovulation is when the egg travels down into the uterus and waits there for 24 hours to be fertilized. Your ovulatory phase is the shortest phase only lasting about 6 days. In actuality you are only fertile for 24 hours because that's how long the egg will remain in your uterus. However there are two factors that make this phase more than just one day, sperm can survive up to 6 days in the body so even if you have sperm in your body from 5 days ago, once the egg hits your uterus, there's the possibility of becoming pregnant. The other factor is that you will never be able to pinpoint the day you will ovulate, but you can make a good prediction and almost certainly confirm it after it has already happened.

Here we have the element of fire and the full moon combined. Imagine a roaring fire, how it cracks and sparks fly from it, this is the element present within you at this time. Or how about the wild wolves that howl up at the full moon? That represents your inner wild nature that wishes to come out and play. This is such a good time to launch, give a presentation, do a photoshoot, keep working on any ideas from your previous phase, your follicular, and to put yourself out there! This phase is like a continuation of your last phase but with more spice so feel free to use this phase to season up your life and your business.

PHASE 4 - *LUTEAL*

Inner Season: *Autumn*

Moon Phase: *Waning Moon*

Elements: *Fire*

Welcome to the last phase of your menstrual cycle! Here in the luteal phase, your progesterone hormone rises, causing the uterine lining to thicken. It does this to prepare for implantation of a fertilized egg.

Progesterone is a hormone that makes you feel good and calms your mood. If there is no fertilization of the egg, progesterone decreases, leading to the uterus shedding its thickened lining which is when your period begins.

You'll notice that the element here is also fire like the previous phase but it's a different kind of fire. The fire of your ovulatory phase is a big roaring fire that doesn't last for very long. Whereas the fire of your luteal phase is a smaller but consistent fire that slowly starts to die down the closer you get to your period. In your first days of your luteal phase you may still feel energized, clear minded, and have the stamina like you did in your previous two phases. Since there is still the element of fire present and your body is preparing to go into an intense ceremony (your period), sometimes there may be feelings of outspokenness and emotional resilience. However, as you get deeper into the luteal phase, your energy can start to dwindle, you may have less patience for things, and you can become more sensitive.

Your luteal phase is known as your inner Autumn because it represents that point where the leaves start to change color and by the end of the season all the leaves have fallen. In the Autumn season there is this in-between where it's still warm enough to be outside but the temperatures begin cooling down. The changing of the leaves color before they fall, mirror your uterine lining thickening before it falls and is released.

The season coincides with the waning moon as it shifts to being more dark in the sky. Remember how during your period we went over how it represents death and darkness? Well this phase is the journey to that.

It can be beneficial at this time to start wrapping things up. Get what you can get done, see what things can be put off until after your period is over, and see how you can get some extra rest to support your body before it bleeds. If you still feel social go out and enjoy! If you still feel clear minded and feel that you can still harness some creativity, work with the energy that is still there. Most importantly, as your energy starts to dwindle, allow yourself to slow down, however that may be realistic to your life.

MOVING FORWARD

I want to put a huge disclaimer and say that not every single menstrual cycle will perfectly align with the moon phases. You could end up bleeding with the full moon and ovulating with the new moon. Please take this and apply it to how it resonates to your life because you may not feel everything that I shared above 100%.

Now where do you go from here with all of this information? Start by noting on your calendar or journal what day your period starts and ends so you know on average how many days you have your period for and how long your menstrual cycle is. It may vary each month. This way you can have a rough idea of where you are in your menstrual cycle. You can take this information and according to which phase you are in, you can apply it to your life in the best way that it works for you. It requires effort to track your cycle but like anything else, once you do it a few times, it becomes second nature.

I like to think of this process as coming back home to yourself and to the innate wisdom of your body. I know when it is a good time for me to host a workshop, launch a service, indulge in social gatherings and when it's time to slow it down and be more introspective all because of my menstrual cycle.

If you are a leader, chances are you are helping to guide others in some way. Leading from the heart means to lead with the organic wisdom that has been embedded within you from the moment you were created inside of the womb. The womb and the heart are related. In fact the womb is actually referred to as the second heart. In Traditional Chinese Medicine there is a channel of energy called the Bao Mai that connects the uterus to the heart space. Just like your heart holds onto memories, emotions, and experiences, so does your womb. Your womb is a major energetic center in the body. Not only does your womb have the capacity to grow a physical life, but it can also help you birth your dreams into existence. Your womb is related to your sexual energy. When I say "sexual energy" I'm not referring to the act of sex but instead the act of creation. Your sexual energy is what helps you to feel connected to your creativity, whatever that may look like for you. Connecting to your menstrual cycle allows you to connect to your womb so that you can lead from both of your hearts.

ALYCIA CAMACHO

Alycia Camacho is an Embodiment Mentor, Certified Personal Trainer, and Spoken Word Artist. Alycia helps women connect to their menstrual cycle so they can learn to live in alignment with their natural fluctuations instead of against them. This is accomplished using education, meditation, breathwork, and movement.

Growing up with various illnesses led her on a pathway of healing holistically and no longer relying on a broken healthcare system. She went on to become a Certified Personal Trainer and study at *The Institute of Integrative Nutrition* to become a health coach. Alycia believes in bridging science with spirituality because both matter. She has taken classes facilitated by doctors and nutritionists in addition to traveling deep into the Amazon rainforest to study with Indigenous spiritual leaders.

Alycia is a New York native with Indigenous ancestral roots from the Caribbean. She enjoys dancing, cooking, hiking, traveling, and being in nature.

Instagram: @alyciacamacho_

HEART MEDICINE

A PRESCRIPTION

It didn't make sense. I did everything like I was supposed to. I had the impressive profession and well paying job with money to spare, but inside I felt blank. Something wasn't right.

Six years into being a pharmacist, I couldn't ignore the feeling of disconnect inside of me anymore. I felt horrible working in a system that focused on managing symptoms of disease rather than curing the disease, and horrible still because the system profited while people were suffering. What I really wanted was to help people feel healthy and vibrant. Working for insurance companies and provider groups proved to be about cutting costs. One of my tasks was to convert elderly patients from once a day insulin injections to multiple injections. The change complicated medication regimens and disrupted disease management that was already stable. Patients stayed sick or got sicker until their body got put into a dire situation and all hope was lost.

I wanted a wellness practice that emphasized change happening from the inside out rather than from the outside in. As a pharmacist, I was literally making suggestions about using medications, a thing outside of ourselves, to change our insides. How could we change from our insides first?

Funny enough, I had to get a dose of my own medicine before I could really help anyone else change from the inside out.

* * *

INSTRUCTIONS

Since before I can even remember, my life seemed laid out for me and crystal clear. I recognized that my immigrant refugee parents made sacrifices for my life to be secure and easy, so in return, I would make them happy and proud by being a pharmacist. This would give them the bragging rights that their daughter is a doctor, the Asian parents' American Dream.

At the same time, like a true Millennial, I changed jobs every two years chasing what was sure to be *The One*. I was blind to the fact that perhaps the root of the problem was actually the profession, since I unconsciously identified as the good, obedient Chinese daughter. During this time of my life, this misguided chasing was only one of the many ways I kept myself stuck.

I also kept myself stuck with the idea that getting married meant I would live happily ever after. I really believed that a relationship with a man and then marriage was the answer to my problems—thanks Disney. It seemed to work for so many of my friends, most of them also pharmacists, happy in their lives. One year I went to seven weddings for goodness sake.

What I didn't consider was that everyone wouldn't be happy under the same circumstances.

* * *

LIVING FROM MY HEART

I'd never had this feeling before. I was in the same house I left a year ago, feeling a familiarity and unfamiliarity sink in at the same time. This is the house I grew up in, but a year full of a lifetime's worth of experiences made for a whole different me.

I left a year ago to travel the world, following my whole heart for the first time in a very long time. All I felt guided by was a desire to travel and write. I had paid off a mountain of student loan debt from undergrad and pharmacy school, and I finally admitted that I didn't want to be a pharmacist, that travel and writing was what I wanted.

Through nineteen countries, I did things I'd never thought I'd do or that are even possible. I was braver than I'd ever been, and more authentic, too.

Because I was following my heart, I found myself doing incredible things I'd never imagined in my life as a pharmacist. I wrote a chapter in a book with my writing group and I got published in an online magazine. I was featured twice on sites about digital nomads. I rode on motorcycles to beautiful cities, beaches, and sights. I enjoyed a retreat in the Sacred Valley of Peru for plant medicine. I played with elephants at a Thai elephant park. I drove a go-kart around Tokyo in a Piglet onesie with my cousin. I hiked a volcano to catch the bright orange sunrise over another volcano in Bali. I bathed in hot springs among the snow-covered Andes at 140 km. I even went scuba diving for the first time, in Cuba of all places.

Being brave came naturally the more I followed my heart because I was having adventures I really wanted. I was brave when I landed in Paris without internet access, not knowing any French and searching for my AirBnB hauling a giant, red travel backpack, eager to immerse myself in the famed city. A jolt of bravery compelled me to jump into the ocean in Dubrovnik, Croatia while the beautiful glowing sun set and my friends called me in after them; and again when jumping off a bridge in Guatapé, Colombia into the water. I felt the bravery in my racing heart when faced with the danger of drowning in a congested river of rafts in Thailand and when I survived Dengue Fever toward the end of my visit in Bali.

I hadn't realized I wasn't authentic until given the chance to be truly authentic. Meeting a whole new group of people allowed for a clean slate. I embraced the chance to lean into my quirky interests and express myself as I knew myself to be rather than being the person the Chinese culture I grew up in told me to be.

I traveled with the same group of people for the whole year as part of a work and travel program. Once I got my bearings with the people I vibed with and what I wanted for my experience that year, I naturally became the group's coach. I led Enneagram and Strengths Finder workshops to encourage self awareness, a monthly storytelling event that fostered bonding, and a fire ceremony with the theme of letting go to let in. These felt close to my heart because people got to know themselves and each other more deeply—a focus on what's inside us (our heart) to connect with what's outside (our world and other people). This felt natural for me and served as glimpses of the work I wanted to do.

I really appreciated that these types of experiences were received well. Much to my delight, other people were also craving heart to heart connections.

***

STUCK

I wasn't sure what 'normal' living was anymore after that year of travel and I fumbled to figure it out.

As soon as I got back to California, I picked up with dating the guy I dated before I left (Let's call him A). Strike one for stuck patterns! I struggled to let go of the amazing chemistry we had, even after dating men who were more considerate and thoughtful toward me. Or maybe I struggled to let go of what I already felt I knew—that he would always want me because he proved it by coming back to me several times even after no contact for a few months. Although this lasted only a short month, I felt gutted because I was in love with him. Stuck patterns will get you if you aren't ahead of them.

Strike two happened when I started a relationship with a guy a few months later (Let's call him B). I repeated a self destructive behavior where I became exactly the lover he wanted. Again, I was so convinced of the promise of happily ever after, that I gave up my own needs and my voice.

I even went back to a pharmacy job. Strike three! Didn't I put in all that effort to get out of pharmacy? But with COVID and the state of everything up in the air, I grasped for security in the area where I felt most confident. Although, I was more conscious about taking the job because of the fact that the income funded my coaching certification. I did tutor for a while, which I love to do, but then subscribed to my mom's belief that tutoring 'isn't a real job.' Again, I forgot my own passions.

To be honest, I lived in ignorance that I had closed off my heart to what I love. This automatic way of living proved much easier than living from my heart because I was so used to it.

* * *

TRUTH SERUM

"I'm not lovable."

I froze in my seat and couldn't even repeat those words. My empowerment coach, Kim, suggested that this belief—I'm not lovable—was causing my problems. When the truth of the words finally registered, my whole body hurt. I hurt deep and wide, stretching from my bones out to my aura. I appreciated that Kim stayed quiet while I sobbed for a while.

This belief really existed inside me. I could sense how believing it affected all of my life up to this point at thirty-four years old. All of my so-called accomplishments were ways I proved to myself and my parents that I could be lovable, that there are reasons to love me. This even extended to my friendships to the tune of 'If I'm like you, then I can be liked too, because you like you.' The bachelor degree, the pharmacy doctorate, the pharmacy residency, the leadership positions, the chasing of a relationship, thing after thing just to prove I'm lovable. But these couldn't fill the hole in my heart.

After that session, I felt raw, as if I had all of my insides exposed to the world to be poked at. And because I was all the wiser now, something had to change.

The nature of healing an untruth like this isn't talked about enough. The process felt like a crazy mess—two steps forward, five steps back, then four steps forward—like a rollercoaster and tripping over my own feet all at the same time.

The relationship with B ended a month later because I finally got honest with myself that I wanted to be a parent and he didn't want kids. I also wanted to be myself—which meant expressing my spiritual side—and he had strong opinions against spirituality.

However, I started up with A again, which went on for an all too long year. That probably kept the part of me who believed "I'm not lovable" affirmed. I was stuck again. Dang those five steps back.

Finding the strength within me took a hell of a lot. I never took to therapy, having all of one asynchronous texting session with a social worker, but at one point I worked with three coaches. One for empowerment, one for life, and one for mindset. Not to mention the weekly practices with my classmate because I was a coach-in-training. I also worked regularly with an energy healer for the first time.

The work of being honest with my heart required that I show up and be resilient. I was finally getting real with my heart which meant feeling a lot of emotions I didn't want to feel. Emotions that had been backlogged since childhood. There was so much crying. Eventually I stopped caring that I cried in public or at the slightest trigger. I sat with a lot of pain I had no idea I was carrying inside. Pain and anger that had to be released. I suppose the dam inside that was all of these feelings finally opened and I had to express it all out of me.

We really can't ignore how we're feeling and I learned that the hard way. Eventually our heart and our needs have to make themselves known because our nervous systems can only carry so much. Also, to feel is to be who we are—human.

* * *

HEALING

Working with my nervous system was the way I would heal from the inside out. It needed lots of TLC after all these years of being in hyperdrive and admittedly, abused and neglected. I committed to daily work because I knew I could feel better and that there was better. My life slowly changed as I deepened my meditation practice, picked up breathwork, and trained in shamanic energy medicine.

With the space to observe my thoughts because of meditation, I understood that I could do things for the simple fact that I wanted to, not because I needed to prove I'm lovable to my parents or friends. So I went to Cape Town when a friend invited me and learned more about healing trauma alongside beach days and intimate conversations with dear friends, which had a healing effect of their own.

I have to emphasize the importance of leaning into a community for support and accountability. Because I had people to turn to when my feelings felt crazy and my heart hurt, I was stronger. These trusted loved ones were able to share their strength in my time of need, which supported me to be resilient. I had to let go of pride that wanted to make changes all by herself, and that took humility. Again, I fumbled as I learned and practiced these new ways of relating to my heart.

As all the feelings and tensions in my body got processed through breathwork, I had space to believe in more of what is possible. For example, I *could* live a lifestyle I wanted. One where my time was my own and I did project-based work. So I resigned from the pharmacy job and went all in with tutoring and coaching. Becoming a committed entrepreneur is a challenge that keeps me working on my inner state and strength every day.

The training in shamanic energy medicine healed parts of myself that I had no idea existed, let alone that needed healing. This opened my eyes to natural talents I had ignored or shut down because I understood them to be weird based on what society decides is 'normal.' All of this work together really inspired me to be in service to others so that they could also be their best and feel better. After all, we can't know what we don't know. Healing and integrating both individual and collective trauma compels me from my heart.

The gradual evolution of "I'm not lovable" shifted to "I'm lovable" and then "I love me." That took about one year. From the security of this in my deep heart, I decided I did want a relationship for it to add to my already great life. I got rid of the happily ever after lie! So I finally told A , 'No,' when he resurfaced after his usual run of one or two months of no contact. Not too long later, a man who is a perfect complement to what I need entered my life. It's so sweet how that works. I feel really lucky.

TODAY

I had been foolish to look anywhere else besides my own heart. Now I was doing everything like I wasn't supposed to because no one else could ever know my heart. And this fool now takes care to commune with her heart, a little every day.

I'm not successful in the way my parents wanted and believed I would be happy with. Yet I'm happy as an entrepreneur trying things out in an unpredictable manner because I like experimenting and learning and I have a lot of fun. I also have more resources than I did before, since I recognize how self care and a community are essential. The people in my communities provide love, support, and expansion, which are really priceless things.

I'm not married because Prince Charming would save me and I'd count on the promise of a happy ending. Rather, I'm in a conscious relationship that I choose, so we get to build and create our joyful life together. Marriage would just be another conscious choice from my heart.

Making changes for ourselves isn't easy, but it's worth it because being stuck gets us nowhere. I'm happier today than I've ever been and I truly am having fun growing up. In fact, I prefer growing up this way—with my heart smiling and feeling fulfilled from the inside out.

HELEN LIM

Helen Lim is a pharmacist turned energetic healer, uplevel coach, and the founder of Helen Coaches. Her work as a healer focuses on creating a space where people feel safe to express themselves and let go of what no longer serves them. She helps people who feel stuck find their strength within so that they can make the changes they've always wanted. Helen's commitment to soul searching, sovereignty, and letting go of mainstream beliefs led her to live life differently. Since focusing on her enjoyment, she traveled the world for a year. Her training includes yoga, meditation, health and life coaching, and shamanism. She is also a podcast host on Awakened…Now What?!, a podcast that illuminates the spiritual awakening journey. She has been featured on Podcast Business News and Freelance Digital Nomad Life Magazine. Notably, she believes compassion changes the world for the better and explores individual and collective trauma integration.

Instagram: @helen_coaches

Linkedin: www.linkedin.com/in/helen--lim/

LIVING VIBRANTLY

I'm often told that I'm lucky. That I am living the dream. The truth is, I've dealt with a lot of pain and failure in my lifetime, which has helped me grow into the person I am today. People don't often see the ugly bits - probably because I've hidden them so well. After all, who likes shining light on the uncomfortable, unpleasant moments in life?

There's someone in my life currently that says, our greatest source of power is our shame. I'm learning that although I've felt so ashamed of my failures in the past, they're also the greatest gifts from which I have drawn the biggest personal growth.

If I appear lucky, it's because I've worked damn hard to get here. Writing this book chapter has proven to be quite the test of bravery - putting myself and my failures out there for the world to judge has taken an extraordinary amount of courage from me. I've had to confront old demons and triggers, relive ego deaths and inner child not-enoughness.

I've chosen to share these failures and adventures in the hopes of inspiring you. To show that despite the struggle it's possible to bounce back and live a life better than initially dreamed. After each fall, we have an opportunity to rise higher, to take ownership of our mistakes and grow through our challenges.

When we are led by our hearts, we are open to experiencing all of life —the good and the bad. There may be plenty to be afraid of, perhaps most of all is the numbing that comes from being paralyzed with fear. Yet if we can surpass the fears and experience life to the fullest, we become limitless. I like to call this being "Rich in Life".

DEFINING MOMENTS

"Get good grades so you can get a good job," cautioned my well-intentioned parents. So I studied hard, got the straight A's and then, the jobs. I was a dedicated and diligent employee, excelling in each role. These 'good jobs' took me down a different path than I had envisioned for my future at that time. As a perfectionist, the last thing you want is to get the sack! I had tried so hard to do everything 'right'. And yet there I was, removed from my first job.

I had just completed a grueling stretch of long days in order to finish a project that had been unceremoniously dumped on me. A few weeks prior, my boss had left me to clean up his and another colleague's paperwork mess while he went on a trip. As he departed, he menaced "You'd better finish this before I return". Of course, I got it done.

I knew I had been taken advantage of and boldly informed him via email that I would like support in the work next time around. It didn't matter the amount of time, sweat, and tears I had given them, or that I was one of the best project managers they had. I got fired for making that request.

It was unsettling, scary and shameful. Voices of reason (notably that of my father) echoed in my head, "I should have just kept my mouth shut. Sucked it up." In hindsight, it was easy to see that this boss and his ego felt threatened by me, because I wasn't going to tolerate his behavior. At the time however, I internalized that I had done something wrong—clearly I must have, I had been fired after all! Subconsciously I took on the belief that if I spoke up when bullied, I would pay the price.

Only one year into my professional life and already a first big crumble.

I carried the fear of failure and the trauma of speaking up into the next job. It burned deep inside me, not fully acknowledged or processed. One day, I shared a spur of the moment idea with a client during a meeting. She loved it so much that she called my boss to re-allocate project funds to this initiative. Sadly he did not welcome my big-picture strategic thinking and a few days later, I was taken to the HR office and given a "Performance Improvement Plan" document (PIP) to sign. I read it and said, "this isn't true". The boss was accusing me of wrongdoings that I hadn't done.

The HR officer sighed, "Brienna just sign it, it's much easier if you just sign it". Reading between the lines, I understood that if I didn't, I'd be let go. My boss wasn't present nor had he previously mentioned any issues. I signed the PIP and kept it sitting next to me at work, a daily reminder that my job was on the line thanks to my creative thinking. I followed the PIP to a T in fear of getting fired again for using my voice.

This PIP reinforced my growing belief that I wasn't allowed to use my voice without permission and that to keep financial security, I had to follow the rules. So I colored inside the lines and at the first opportunity, requested to move to another department. I had to get out from under that ego-driven boss. How could I trust him after that sly, passive aggressive move? Was this really how all leaders behaved, so ego-centric? Did they have zero empathy? I didn't feel safe because I couldn't be myself. New ideas, curiosity, open communication and collaboration were not welcomed. I felt my confidence eroding daily…crumble number two.

In the next department, I was a star employee. I managed the largest project in the organization. The client was so happy and in awe of me —in their 30+ years in the industry, they'd never seen anyone work so efficiently or get consultants on board as quickly as I did. One day I asked for a promotion and was denied, simply because I didn't have a Master's degree.

This was the final crumble and the end of buying into corporate politics for me. Regardless of the results I produced or the happy clients I fostered, self-censorship was limiting my growth. My values were compromised and it was time to find those that would cherish my gifts. I led myself with my heart out that door, walking away without a safety net, but with a level of self-trust and knowing that I deserved better.

It was a bold move and also what I needed to do for my nervous system. Years of always being on alert to watch what I said and did had left me fried. Trauma in the workforce is real.

MY MENTORS

I considered going for my Master's and started looking at an MBA program at Stanford. I decided that San Francisco was more my personality. Work there isn't as much about politics as it is about innovation and disruption. Clearly, I had disruption in my blood and evidence to prove this from my previous work experiences!

I wanted to make an impact.

Once in San Francisco I joined a Business Accelerator run by a well known entrepreneur who has been featured on the cover of New York Times. He is known for shaking up the venture capital industry and to me, he embodies disruption and authenticity. He believed in me in a way I'd never encountered before.

With his guidance I learned to embrace imperfection. There's no time to be a perfectionist - launch and pivot as needed, get to work and get seen. He introduced us to several of his successful friends who were also innovative and disruptive. I loved it all! I felt I had found my tribe and began to happily create a new life for myself. Until…

My grandfather developed Alzheimer's and I went back home to help care for him. We were very close. He was a successful entrepreneur and one of my greatest role models. He had come from Mexico without any formal education and made it 'big' in the US, with a handful of hotels and a car for every day of the week to prove it. Before his dementia, we had traveled to Argentina, Chile, Brazil, Uruguay, and all over Mexico. He called me his buddy. I loved learning about entrepreneurship from him and about being bold and audacious. Around him, I didn't feel like I failed when I spoke up but rather, that I was strong and daring. I called him abuelito, an endearing way to say grandfather in Spanish.

One afternoon before his Alzheimer's began, he and my aunt's mother-in-law, a devout Christian, were on the patio together. She asked him "what's new?" He replied "I went to hell". She was all flustered because of what he'd said. Clearly, he was losing his mind! I let the family know that I had taken him to a nightclub where the dancers were wearing devil horns. This wasn't a demented moment, he was speaking of going clubbing with me! He liked to stir the pot, and I'm grateful to him for teaching me to speak up and push some edges.

Abuelito was the reminder of my roots, that bravery and innovation are in my blood. My San Francisco mentor pushed me to dream big and helped rebuild my confidence after the ego shattering corporate experiences. And my current mentor speaks to my heart with living brave.There's a magnetic pull to her vulnerability, radical self-expression and self-acceptance guiding me to new levels of bravery!

MY EVOLUTION

My grandfather passed after several years and I decided a beach vacation was exactly what I needed. I went to Playa del Carmen. I thought I'd spend the summer there before returning to California to continue mentorship with my San Francisco mentor.

That summer in Mexico turned into four years and a three and a half year long relationship. It was the catalyst for me realizing the power of long term travel as a tool to recharge and explore my passions. I let go of many unhealthy workaholic tendencies. I surrendered to the joys of yoga and sunrise paddle boarding. I developed deeper connections in my relationships and lived experiences that challenged me to grow. I learnt that there is more to life than financial success. My priorities became happiness and fulfillment over achieving material abundance.

It was then that I discovered one of my passions—showing people how to embrace long-term travel and use it for their own self-awareness and discovery. Travel is a wonderful way to invigorate your energy. It adds color to life and allows you a chance to paint outside the lines. When you go to a new country, you can be whoever you want. It places you outside of your comfort zone as you come up against new problems, build resiliency and a growth mindset. When you travel to developing countries you learn how easy it is to be happy with very little.

From Mexico, my heart led me to Colombia and then Asia. I have traveled for eleven years now and lived in eleven different countries, following my intuition on where to go next. I learned before the pandemic how to work remotely. Adventures, newness and challenges were what kept my life buzzing with excitement. I love learning about other cultures and ways of living.

If you've ever been to Mexico I'm sure you know, things move at a much slower pace and without the "I need it now" instant gratification attitude of the demanding USA. If you want to learn about patience, go to Mexico.

Asia is very different from the Western world and I've learned a lot from being in environments different from my upbringing. I was scared to go to Vietnam. I thought "how could the Vietnamese not hate us Americans after the war"? It turned out to be one of my favorite Asian countries and the Vietnamese embrace Americans with hospitality and love. If you want to learn about forgiveness, go to Vietnam.

Bali was my home during the pandemic. Highlights of my time there included afternoons in the garden, admiring the floral arrangements made by my gardener, receiving powerful blessings as my Balinese friends prayed for me and my family, and having one of the Balinese Kings ask me to marry his son! If you want to learn about faith and surrender, go to Bali.

FACING FEARS

I have so many travel stories and experiences that would never have happened had I stayed working in the comfort of a corporate 9-5 office job. Every time I went to a new place, I was met with new challenges - my ways of being and beliefs, tested. There is great growth to be found in discomfort and a powerful way to recalibrate pain, is to face fear.

Those initial bosses propelled me onto a different path where I got to confront my fears and experience an expanded growth mindset, freedom, independence and resilience. I'm grateful for that.

I am afraid of dogs (I've been bitten on two occasions) and in Bali, dogs are everywhere—on the beach, in the restaurants, at the gym, at the temples, EVERYWHERE. I would have been very limited in where I could go had I not learned to manage this fear.

I am afraid of heights but I've managed to climb up some really steep stairs and rickety ladders in order to see the best views around the world.

I am afraid of needles and yet went for an acupuncture session in order to tackle a constant migraine issue I was having.

I don't, however, fear death, because I've lived and experienced so much. I'm not sure I'd feel the same had I remained behind an office desk this whole time. Through travel, my courage is tested all of the time. If you want to find fearlessness, travel more.

THE GIFTS...

HEART-CENTERED LEADERSHIP

In my time in corporate, my colleagues and I did not have a lot of emotional intelligence and empathy was sorely lacking all around. I have since learned that empathy is a superpower that brings people together and increases productivity and happiness in the workplace. The gifts I received inspired me to be a heart-centered leader in my own coaching practice and to model empathy for others.

I now focus on teaching others how to lead with empathy, how to listen rather than judge, how to lift people up instead of tear them down, how to choose curiosity over criticism. I help my clients identify their Saboteurs (the ego's inner critics) that stop them from living their best lives and leading productive, happy teams. By becoming aware of the Saboteurs, leaders can shift from fear and ego to love and empathy.

SOUL ALIGNED SUCCESS

In my time in corporate, I lost sight of my values, censoring myself and sacrificing my confidence in order to fit the mold. I have since learned that soul-aligned success means living a life of purpose and intention that is entirely personal to each individual. The gifts I received were to surround myself with people who inspire me to be self-expressed and to step out of my comfort zone.

I now focus on teaching that life is abundant and misery is optional. I help my clients to design a life of increased happiness and fulfillment, to live vibrantly and authentically. By being present and appreciative, leaders can tap into their Sage energy and find peace and calm.

MY LIBERATION

In my time in corporate I was not accepted for who I really was. I have since learned that self-acceptance is critical to personal responsibility and freedom. Accepting myself as I am also makes it easier for me to allow others to be as they are. The gifts I received were to expand my horizons and discover a wider range of people and cultures to embrace. I now focus on using travel as a tool for expansion and appreciation of contrast. I help my clients to be brave and explore. By facing their fears, leaders build resilience to life's challenges, develop trust in self and amplify their sense of freedom.

PARTING WORDS

In the Japanese art of Kintsugi, gold is placed in the cracks of mended pottery. The idea is that something "broken and ugly" can not only be made beautiful again, but even increase in value and desirability thanks to its perceived flaws. It treats breakage and repair as part of the noble history of an object, to be celebrated rather than disguised or rejected.

As we lead with our hearts from a place of vulnerability, we expose ourselves to potentially being broken, revealing weakness and imperfection. We can choose to give up and abandon the pieces, or pick them up and repair them, using the opportunity to alchemize life's painful moments into golden gifts, each time creating new layers of history to treasure, appreciate and transform into an upgraded work of art, "Rich in Life".

BRIENNA BECKER

Brienna Becker is a Certified Positive Intelligence and trauma-informed coach as well as a Leader, Visionary and Change Catalyst. She mentors accomplished technology leaders to have more empathy and to create more space for joy. She also works with teams to develop a corporate culture of trust, collaboration and mutual accountability. This cultivates teams that thrive and individuals who feel "rich in life".

Being rich in life is a state of peace, happiness and fulfillment. Brienna is a cheerleader for you to live to your fullest potential! Her mission is to help her clients design a life led by passions rather than fears and she facilitates them through this process as the founder of "Digital Nomads: Rich in Life". Her superpower is empathy.

Brienna has lived as a digital nomad for 11 years in 11 different countries. Travel is her favorite tool for recharging and self-exploration.

Website: www.DigitalNomadsRichinLife.com

LinkedIn: www.linkedin.com/in/briennamichelle

Facebook: www.facebook.com/briennamichelle

Instagram: @briennamichelle8

HOW MY HEART WAS INFLUENCED BY NATURE AND SPORTS

"Leadership is influence, nothing more, nothing less."

- John C. Maxwell

I am convinced that we are all born with an ability to lead. Some of us are brought into leadership at an early age and others discover the capability later on in life. Either way, like my mentor Mr. Maxwell shares, it comes down to a simple principle; *influence*. How are you able to influence yourself towards a greater vision than your reality currently holds and how are you able to influence others towards a place they deeply desire to go? Combine that with the power of the heart, an electromagnetic generator connected to the field of innate wisdom that has the ability to *know* and *influence* before the rational mind can even process, one is guided by the harmony of the interstitial depths of the quantum Universe that many refer to as "God".

In this chapter, I intend to share how I was able to extract wisdom from my experiences early on in life through Nature and Athletics that guided me to traveling the world and opening up multiple businesses where I have the honor to lead others back to their own place of heart-centered leadership through transformational health practices and business models that focus on the upliftment of the earth and humanity.

As far back I can remember, there were two things that consumed me and helped create me: Nature and sports.

In nature is where I began to tap into the existential peace of the world around me. Many times a year I was given the ability to learn how to drop into the heart and shut out the noise from societal constructs that were deeply programming my mind. Because here's the deal, the subtle messages of television, bombardment of advertisements, the fixation of video games, and even the systems built upon "sit still, memorize, regurgitate and be like everyone else" really works. It certainly affected a sensitive empath like me and possibly even yourself…

I have discovered it's imperative to find ways to break that conditioning and influence of mind. Because here's the deal, your mind is here to observe and be in awe! Which it will do when given enough of any stimuli. So, what stimuli do you want to inject, focus on and be influenced by?

Fortunately, on a hidden little trout stream where my parents conceived me, I first learned to sink into the songs of heart and the sounds of life. Here I was able to observe the 'Real World'. It all felt so true, where life had been existing so intuitively for millions and millions of years. In nature, one is able to observe how life is existing - not to constantly compete, out build, outdo and out-be the rest - rather to live in harmony with one another; cooperating, connecting, playing, respecting the cycles of life and living in what seemed to be ultimate joy, love and gratitude - to me. And with this pure observation of the Real World, I found I was able to also tap deeply into *my* Real World.

Before I ever knew what meditation was, my father was teaching me the essence of being still, stealthy and aware of what was going on within and around me. In order to be the best at this thing I was consumed with and influenced by, I had to develop a high level of awareness to move and be "One" with nature. Aside from the phrases of "Shhhh, you'll spook the trout.." and "Let him run! Don't horse him in.."—that I would later bestow upon my friends who ventured along —I observed the grace of my father while fishing. I became a student of his every move and an executor of his every word and was enamored that one could be so stoic doing what seemed to be so little. It felt like his presence would merge with the world around him where time and space no longer made a difference. It was in those moments of adoration where I first began to understand peace.

On top of that, I quickly learned that when I had a lot on my mind while trying to fish, I would either make a bad cast, get tangled up in a tree or a fish would break off because I was "horsing" it in. It was almost as if everything that was happening in my subconscious reality would rise up for me to work through while on the river. And when I made peace with it, I was able to drop back into the present moment, find the joy of where I was and more often than not met with a "WHAM". Fish on!

With this paramount education into life, I became inspired to invite friends along on fishing trips year after year. Before I knew it, I found myself guiding and leading them in a way that would impact many of their lives in the ways it did for me. We all had the opportunity to "find ourselves" on the river, hiking many miles away on our own, spending the entire day fishing upstream, exploring the mysteries of life and connecting with the spirit of earth and our hearts. I started to refine the ability to teach what my father was passing down to me; how to clean a fish, where to cast the bait for an almost guaranteed hook in, the importance of being a steward of the land, how to slow down and be patient in a world of instant gratification and most of all, how to *listen*.

I've come to discover that there is something profound and mystical about nature. When one is able to sit with the culminated harmonics of birds singing, water rushing over rocks and the wind blowing through the trees, it settles us into a grand sense of peace. When we are able to destress and exit the monkey mind of past or future thought and simply be, we are able to *feel*—for if we want to *feel better*, we must get *better at feeling*. When we are in presence and at peace; we are able to witness the goosebumps rising on our skin—which I consider are the *whispers* of God. When we are able to access this state of divinity—ideas far beyond our logical mind from books or people are able to come through and we can tune into the sagacity of those who came before us—for they *knew* how to work with the mysticism and heart wisdom we all behold.

In a world where we are so affected by listening to everyone else and little to ourselves, there were times on the river where no one would speak. Imagine three to five young teenagers (sometimes more) all completely silent, immersed, stoked—doing what others would think is so little and boring. Yet, here we were studying at the school of Heart. I remember having some of the most profound conversations of my life down on the river with my friends.

On a hot summer day, after we had each pulled a few fish out of a big hole, we all sat down on a dead log that laid parallel with the river upon the bank before we continued upstream. This tree had probably been there longer than we had been alive and had the feeling of many others before us who also sat here gazing at the coniferous trees above, wondering how long had this river been carving out this canyon of steeping sand banks.

At that moment someone asked, "what do you guys think God is?".

To which one of us responded, "This."

Silence ensued as we all gazed around in awe. "Yeah, this." we all agreed in solitude.

It was then, at the age of fifteen where I confirmed that nature was my church. It was my place of reverence and reprieve. It was the place where I could not just go and speak to the essence of heart and love, it's where I learned to speak and listen in, even while I was embedded in the inundation of others and the density of social conditioning. Honestly, at the time it didn't seem like much. It felt normal and true. And as I look back, it was all of that time in nature - disconnected from the pressurizing frequent inundation of humans and the density of other electromagnetic frequencies which allowed me to drive a neural groove of heart focused *influence* into my system that couldn't be undone. It's as if once you put on that lens of heart you can never go back to the things as they are with a blind eye.

In fact, every time I would come back to the city after even a short three day retreat into nature, the whole world looked different. I had more empathy for the people around me. I was less stressed, anxious and depressed. I found myself energized, present, able to see the pain, the doubt, the worry and shame within others just as I felt it in myself. I also saw the worth, potential and amazingness that we all held just waiting to be fully owned. And ultimately, I began to see how well all of us were influenced by others without really even knowing it. So, I chose to be of influence to those around me for good in all that I could. This influence subconsciously drove me to be a better human. I felt that the world would be a better place if others had also experienced what I got to experience. Of course, I couldn't take everyone with me, however I could treat everyone and everything with the same type of respect and kindness that Nature treated me with. So that is what I began to do. And the big training grounds for this stage of my life was in athletics.

When I wasn't fishing on the river, I was playing sports around the neighborhood. From street football, to backyard baseball, to capture the flag, to even racing against friends and family to see who was the fastest. I was greatly influenced by my obsession with sports and performance.

From the ages of 10 to 23, I competed heavily in baseball, basketball and football where I slowly and assuredly learned how to optimize my skills and abilities through fitness, nutrition, mindset, breath and leadership. In truth, nearly every team I played for I was elected team captain by my peers—a gift that positioned me early on to share these insights with you. I also had the fortune of fulfilling my dream of playing collegiate baseball after overcoming what I eventually called a "catalyzing" knee injury in which the doctor told me I would no longer be able to continue my endeavors to play at the next level. I discovered the physical aspects of leadership in resiliency, determination and discipline. All the while uncovering the intangibles like creating deep connections with teammates, instilling unshakeable belief and trust within self and others and simply put, becoming the greatest version of self.

Of course to compete at a collegiate level I was required to have a high level of skill, which I humbly worked upon year in and year out, never arrogantly *expecting* to be a shoe in to any team I played for yet at the same time I always *believed*. And that belief was curated by passionately working upon my craft day in and day out, being a student of the game and a student of life.

From the outside in I feel and think a lot of people consider leaders as those who are simply the best at what they do. And I am here to tell you it's much more than that and to be elected team captain or considered a leader in anything you do requires something much more than skill alone.

Sure, you can be highly talented and athletically gifted and that will get you to a certain place or level in life. However, what happens when you're not in the game? Or when you're unable to work on your business because you have a family emergency? Or you have to leave the family for an unexpected work trip? The best leaders aren't those who people *rely on*. They are the ones who create a container for others to lead *themselves*. Therefore, if you can lead through connection, empowerment and emotion along with the physical determination and discipline, you are able to create *trust* and *belief* in others to rally around a common mission and goal to learn and win.

In this shifting paradigm of leadership I think we can all agree that it is so much more than bossing people around and just being the best.

Sure, those could be aspects of 'leadership' but personally I don't really care how good you are if you cannot connect with me and I am even far less receptive if you're an asshole about it. What I acquired and intuitively leaned into throughout my athletic career was to..

1. Lead by example in discipline, determination and growth
2. Create real, honest and even vulnerable connections with the people you are surrounded by

I played with many great athletes who failed to create connections with teammates let alone talk to them. They had all of the tools in the world; strong, athletic and talented without trying. Yet, they weren't well received by other guys because they would put teammates down, call them names, joke about them repeatedly, expect players to be just as good as them and perpetually made it about themselves.

I played with guys who could connect with anyone. They were likable and empathetic but lacked the motivating drive and discipline to lead by example. They weren't someone you could get behind and run through a brick wall with because you didn't think *they* would actually do it. They merely "talked a good game".

Then, there were the few athletes that brought it all together. They may not have been the best "athletically", but they outworked everyone else. They were dedicated to their mission. They embodied patience, sat in trust, had unshakeable belief and understood delayed gratification. They found time to get to know everyone and ask the harder questions. They weren't shy about opening up and sharing deeper parts about themselves. They made you feel safe and seen. You were motivated by their presence and willing to lay it on the line because you had this leader "going up to bat" with you, ready to run through that proverbial brick wall. And the teams that consisted of this type of overall leadership were by far the most successful of them all.

I share this from the perspective of my own point of view, because they were the traits and characteristics that I admired and was most influenced by in the leaders I played with early on and was mentored under in life and business. It made sense. It resonated. It resonates. So I followed suit as I continued to find myself in leadership positions and have now molded it into my own way that fits me.

The lessons and experiences I have absorbed through Nature and Athletics have been foundational in supporting my journey through leading myself and others. Because of my deep connection and desire to be in nature, I decided to travel the world with merely a backpack and a partner adventuring in the far stretches of the world for months at a time, to then acquiring sponsorships from a couple of fly fishing brands and outdoor gear companies to spend a few months trout fishing around Nebraska and Backpacking in Colombia. This then led me to starting a business where I have helped guide and transform the health and wealth of over 1,200 individuals (and rapidly growing) nourishing the body at the cellular level all while focusing on environmental stewardship and working with regenerative farmers around the world. On top of that, doors have opened up to lead and co-facilitate nature based transformational retreats and I have been asked to step into the Men's Embodiment work, supporting brothers from around the world to release the shame, fear and doubt while stepping into a Man who leads with honesty, vulnerability, strength and integrity.

As an athlete, I was determined to earn my way onto the playing field, be the best athlete I could be and support my teammates in the best ways I learned how. Now, I've become determined to be the best leader that I can be in life and in business whilst inspiring and guiding others to lead themselves through their own journey with ultimate health. I've learned it requires unshakeable belief, an attunement to the natural world and a willingness to do what may seem is most challenging and uncomfortable. And I believe you can be that type of leader too! Don't get me wrong, I still have my own fears and doubts that pop up from time to time. Challenges inevitably arise and I question my self worth and capability. Then, I get out into nature. I bask in the stillness and peace of life, am reminded of the awe and capability we are born with and reattune to the heart's existential wisdom, belief and desire.

I lead from there.

And, in my experience, if you too lean into this, you will lead yourself towards a once unimaginable reality that simply started out as your heart's dream and many will be inspired to lead themselves through the doors of Heart with courage and trust alongside your magnetizing, influential spirit..

> "You can't change people, you can only inspire them to change themselves."
>
> - Elon Musk

JOHN PAUL KINGSTON

John Paul, the founder of JPK Experience, is a Men's Embodiment and Transformation Coach who guides groups and individuals back to their hearts through health, wealth, love and happiness. John Paul focuses on helping people clear their body through nutritional guidance, somatic release, emotional wellness, inner-child work and soul connection to liberate from the deeply conditioned mind and back to what the heart is calling for.

At an early age he found himself in many leadership positions through his athletic endeavors all the way up to his collegiate baseball tenure. It wasn't skill alone that got him nominated consistently as team captain; he always leaned on connection and inclusivity. This focus led him to backpacking around the world, leading adventure wellness retreats, building a superfood business responsible for nearly $1 million in sales in 3 years, facilitating Men's Circles in the US and Mexico all while leading thousands of people to live healthier, wealthier and whole.

Website: www.jpkexperience.com

Facebook: www.facebook.com/thejpkexerience/

Instagram: @jpkexperience

REVOLUTIONIZING HEART CENTERED HEALTHCARE

WHAT IS HEART CENTERED LEADERSHIP?

The heart in eastern medicine is the center. It defines our soul, our connection with others. Its energy is outward and expansive, it vibrates and emits energy around our entire body. In eastern medicine the health of the heart is reflected in the eyes because it is said that they are the windows to the soul. Our eyes, when depressed reflect dullness, when the eyes are bright it means connection to our purpose or WHY. The heart reflects the fire element representing our body's metabolism, the emotion of joy and our desires. The heart pathway within us defines who we are authentically. When it comes to being a heart centered leader I believe that if we come from a place of love and service we create expansion in our community. A leader should be one that leads through compassion and understanding that all beings are connected, and what we do on this earth, even small acts can create a ripple effect of change within our communities. We are all leaders in our own right. When you find what lights you up, your passion, and you find a way to use that passion to contribute to enhancing others, you are a heart centered leader that is living out your purpose. There is no better feeling than knowing you can contribute to enhancing the lives of others. Your purpose defines the WHY for your mission in life. My WHY is to expose eastern medicine to the masses and create a revolution in our healthcare system, so that people have a choice when it comes to their medicine.

Did you know that most people over forty are taking at least four kinds of medication daily?

The pandemic in particular created a forty percent increase in opioid and anxiety medication use. Most of these people stay on these medications the rest of their life without really knowing any other way, and sometimes ultimately suffering the consequences of the long term side effects of the drugs.

I am here to tell you that you have options when it comes to your health.

Eastern medicine has been around for centuries, and it focuses on addressing the root cause of disease.

In this chapter I will tell you my story of how I overcame debilitating health concerns through eastern medicine, as well as how being a heart centered leader helped me to create a multi- practitioner, multi-disciplined, acupuncture and holistic wellness center which has been open since 2012.

My intention is to empower others to be advocates in their own healthcare, as well as empower leaders in my industry to be confident in healing the masses so that they can continue the mission of mainstreaming heart centered healthcare. I will be telling you about the vast differences in the East vs West, and why both medicines need to work together, as well as give you some insight on my proprietary way of operating my team oriented wellness center.

MY STORY OF ACUPUNCTURE

It all started when I became a martial artist. I hold a black belt in TaeKwonDo and would compete in sparring. The asian culture has always interested me, and my personality is always one that loves thinking outside the box.

During one of my competitions I sprained my ankle. A traditional MD told me that in order to heal, to stop training in TaeKwonDo for six months. This was pretty devastating for me as I spent more than six hours daily training and working there. My instructor told me to try acupuncture. I went for two to three sessions, and from there, I was back competing within just a couple of weeks. That was a defining moment that made me decide to obtain my masters degree in eastern medicine.

Upon enrolling in Acupuncture school I was having a hard time focusing, and went through swings of depression and also having anxiety. After a psychiatrist's diagnosis of Complex Post Traumatic Stress Disorder (C-PTSD) from childhood trauma, I was given medication. I reluctantly took it, but I did feel the medication helped me level out and be able to function in everyday life.

After six months of being on medication I was diagnosed with hypothyroidism. Physically I was very fit, I was a martial artist, and exercised five to six days per week. The only change in my life was that medication. The diagnosis led me down a rabbit hole of internet searching on forums of other people that developed hypothyroidism from taking this medication. My psychiatrist and MD told me they had never heard of such a thing. I decided to try acupuncture, and with the help of my doctors, was able to wean off of the medication entirely.

Another way acupuncture helped me was for my menstrual cycle. At a young age I was put on birth control because I would have black out migraine headaches and an irregular and painful cycle. Birth control helped the symptoms, but gave me mood swings. Yet another medication that did help me, but also gave me other problems. Acupuncture solved that.

In school I learned so much about how versatile this medicine was, and knew that it could help so many people. I was really frustrated at the approach of western medicine not giving me real answers while putting me on medications with no impending end date. I was told It was just something I was going to have to deal with for the rest of my life. It saddened me that even with help in western medicine, it created other problems for me. Now with regular acupuncture, meditation, exercise and maintaining a healthy diet I have a regular and normal period without PMS. I no longer have the diagnosis of hypothyroidism, and I do not need to take antidepressants or anxiety medication.

It was from my own personal story that I knew that I needed to improve the way of healthcare, and expose people to ALL options when it comes to taking care of our bodies and minds. I wish I had known about this medicine sooner.

HOW OUR SYSTEM NEEDS TO BE IMPROVED, EAST VS WEST, AND HOW WE CAN WORK TOGETHER

In my opinion our healthcare system is broken. Many of the people that try the mainstream western approach who seek help for injuries and sickness, will end up staying sick. Unfortunately in the USA doctors get paid as long as their patients are sick. Pharmaceutical companies sell their products and doctors get perks and benefits on selling those drugs. I am not going to say there is always something wrong with pharmaceuticals, the truth is that there is a time and place and like I shared in my story, medication helped me. Medication is not the problem, the problem is that people do not know there is a choice.

Some other things I experienced in my western medicine doctors' offices is to wait an hour or more to be seen, only for them to spend minutes with me, I felt like a number. I believe medicine should be about holding space for patients. As a practitioner, I found that healing happens when you allow the patient to be able to express themselves. Eastern medicine focuses a lot on the emotions behind the disease and the physical ailment behind it, something that western medicine may not consider.

Even with eastern medicine becoming more mainstream I am not sure that all acupuncturists come from a heart centered place either. Since we can bill insurance, it is common for practitioners to overbook their schedule, spend little time with their patients, and do minimal acupuncture needles with no real diagnosis. We call this puppy mill acupuncture. Make sure you see a practitioner that can properly educate you on points they choose and why. You have a right to understand what is being done to your body. It's our job as practitioners to teach you about this medicine, not keep you in the dark. There is only so much we can do in the treatment room, the more tools we can educate you on to help yourself between sessions, only contributes to the success of your treatments. A good acupuncturist will want to educate you.

Despite the improvements I would like to see in the western approach, I do feel there is absolutely a place for western medicine. I would never tell someone that was in a car accident and bleeding out to go get acupuncture. Western medicine is amazing for its emergency medicine. It also has tools and the latest technology of machines to diagnose. I do not know where we would be without the modernization of western medicine.

In my practice, I come from a place of reflecting on my work by executing evaluations and reevaluations. I want to know that what I am doing is actually helping that patient. Tools like blood work, MRIs, CT scans, or x-rays that western medicine provides can be crucial in measuring the healing process. Even as an eastern medicine practitioner, understanding these images and being able to use them in practice is crucial for bridging the gap with western medicine practices. Eastern medicine mainly relies on patterns related to the five element systems which we will talk about later.

As a leader, I found that having systems in place that allow for measurable goals, and a time and space to reflect and measure those goals, creates healthier and happier patients, and more successful practitioners. I am not a person to do something without knowing its cause and effect. Evaluations and reevaluations are crucial in the success of healing.

Although I operate like a western medicine practice with measurable goals, eastern medicine is my main focus. It is a complete and whole medicine that is separate from western medicine. It is not better than western medicine, it is just different. We diagnose differently, and how we treat depends on the patterns we see in a patient's body. We understand patterns through the questions we ask them, as well as what we feel in their pulse, and what we see looking at their tongue. The biggest difference is that we look at the body as a whole. Each system works together as small parts to a bigger whole. When one of the systems is off balance it can affect the other systems. Acupuncture is a general practice, in the east we do not only just consider the physical health of the person, we also consider the mental, emotional and spiritual health of a person.

If you want immediate relief, western medicine is better at this, but over time there may be some harsh consequences from them. Eastern medicine may take longer for you to heal but it has more lasting effects and less side effects. Unfortunately it is not a magic pill that you can take that will allow you to get miraculously better.

Eastern medicine is very similar to losing weight, or gaining more muscle, you can't go to the gym to workout one time and expect to achieve that goal immediately. Each session will build onto the next, and goals are accomplished overtime. Depending on how long you have had a condition, helps us determine the amount of treatments that might be needed to achieve your goal. This medicine is pretty amazing and can do great things, I have known for a majority of the patients in the practice to get relief after just a few sessions. But the biggest mistake my patients make is that if they are feeling better they stop treatment. It is a mistake because we didn't spend the time strengthening their body so that they are able to maintain the endurance to stay that way. The ultimate goal is to get every patient to a place where they are getting tune up treatments—just like your car needs oil and maintenance, your body needs those as well, even if you are feeling good. After all, this medicine was originally used as preventive medicine. Most of my patients, even if they are feeling good, come one time a month to four times per year, and this generally keeps them in check to stay healthy and vital along with the tools and education we provide them with to maintain and understand where their bodies strengths and weaknesses are.

Eastern medicine is an individualized medicine, meaning two people can come in with the same complaint, but may be treated differently based on their constitution, the root, their symptoms and their branch. As acupuncturists we are energy detectives. We have tools to uncover patterns of imbalance within the body. There is a minimum of five years of schooling to become an acupuncturist, and we extensively study the body when it comes to both western sciences and eastern philosophy. We need to understand the anatomy as well as the pathway in which our metabolism flows through the body, where and how Qi will pool, and where imbalances happen that can make people sick. We help to uncover the strengths and weaknesses of our patients and can identify their patterns of imbalance.

BEING A LEADER IN THE EASTERN MEDICINE WORLD

My job as a practice owner with multiple therapists is to understand and know the strengths and weaknesses of my team. We are all categorized in different archetypes, just like there are different seasons that make the world go round, there are unique individuals that come together as a team to make a successful practice. Being able to bounce cases and ideas together is part of our success. In a community there are different unique parts to each individual that contribute to the whole of a bigger picture. Just how eastern medicine works for the body, eastern philosophy can be used in applying leadership. It is important that you know and understand your team.

Being a heart centered leader in my experience is a lot like being a mom. It is my responsibility to hold my team accountable in operating in a way that not only helps others but helps themselves. I want not only my kids, but also my patients and team to learn, grow and thrive. They must have an understanding of their values and moral compass. It might be easy to just allow our kids or team to do whatever they want, chaos can ensue without rules and structure.

What provides clarity and structure in my team is having a set of core values. Mine are Integrity, Compassion, Education, Team work, Accountability, and Communication. These core values are the template in which I operate my life and my practice. If things do not fit into these set of core values, I know that it is not going to work. They are important to refer to in maintaining my company culture and knowing if potential team members would be a fit to help revolutionize this medicine. We all have a similar WHY, and that is modernizing and mainstreaming this medicine in order to provide a choice in healthcare. Through the different element archetypes, we each play a unique role in contributing to that goal. As a leader it's my job to know my team's five element archetype.

I am an earth element constitution. Earth is the central pivot and in the body it represents the digestive system, groundedness, and it is the nourisher. Earths are typically very generous, and love the sense of community, they nourish all the other elements by providing the nutrients in order for the other elements to thrive.

I have other team members that are fire—my office manager. Fire nourishes the earth from the ash that provides soil, in other terms, the fire supports the earth's growth.

Metal element is my lead acupuncturist: Metal element is all about creating a container, and understanding the detail and the more subconscious type of medicine. Metals tend to be super organized and thrive on structure. Metal is created from the earth so my leadership helps to nourish him and thrive in creating structure in the practice. With structure comes creation.

Each of the element archetypes play a role into a successful practice. That is why my model of building successful acupuncture practices includes collaboration. If you would like to know what your archetype is, take my 5 element archetype quiz posted on my site.

As a leader in my industry I learned to be super clear on my message as well as the expectations I have for my team in order to have success in the practice. Having things written down and as spelled out as possible always leaves less room for misinterpretation on the goals and expectations of each member in the team. When everyone knows their role and has agreed to the conditions of their job, it's just better in the long run.

Creating a movement and culture means as a leader practicing what I preach and also holding myself accountable. Self care and communication are incorporated into my team meetings. Allowing space for the communication to happen regularly in scheduled team meetings is important for maintaining a healthy team culture.

Being a leader requires continued growth. Just like the patients we treat in eastern medicine, without change, we are stuck and stagnant. Growth and healing does not happen. The hope is that we are always evolving and improving our skills and our health, that is why once a month during our team meetings we have dedicated times for continued education, group meditations, process practicing, and statistical analysis. Healing and growth happens in a nurturing reflective container that allows for a safe collaborative effort. The investment of the belief that the collective mind is always better than the singular mind has been a major factor in maintaining success in my heart centered practice, and also how we've been able to properly educate our patients in finding answers for their own preventive healing.

My hope is that with more successful acupuncturists, and more education in eastern medicine, we can help to modernize this amazing medicine and allow people to feel empowered to become advocates of their own healthcare again. Will you join me in the continued effort to revolutionize heart centered healthcare? I would love to hear from you.

ELIZABETH MARTIN

Elizabeth M. Martin L.Ac, is a Licensed Acupuncturist and Chinese Medicine Mentor, who empowers people to overcome trauma. Her mission is to modernize holistic medicine, bridge the gap between eastern and western medicine, and give people a choice when it comes to their healthcare. In her private practice, Hands On Acupuncture and Massage Therapy PC, Elizabeth leads her team of medical freedom fighters.

Learning through her own childhood emotional trauma, Elizabeth believes in guiding others to heal themselves for the sake of their future generations. By combining Chinese medicine, self care, personal development, and meditation, she teaches and empowers others to become advocates in their own preventative care both online and in person. Elizabeth is a mother of two boys and spends her free time traveling with them in their converted school bus (skoolie). She's been featured in media such as Modern Mom, Good + Well, open fit, Motherhood Maternity and more.

Website: www.HandsOnAcupuncture.com

Website: www.ElizabethMMartin.com

Instagram: @mindful_momprenuer

Facebook: Elizabeth Martin

HEARING THE WHISPERS OF THE HEART

The gifts held in each of our hearts are reflected back to us in the magical synchronicity embodied by nature. These are the whispers of the worlds of the heart that remind us we are seen; we are heard and we are the space holders of the healing waiting to find each beautiful wild heart.

* * *

BEFORE YOU SETTLE in to read the words that have poured from my heart to these pages, I ask you to take a deep breath and allow yourself to drop into this moment. As you exhale, imagine yourself in your late twenties. Then allow yourself to hear that you are as exasperating as a wild horse; unpredictable, untamable and unlovable spill from the lips of the man you love. Part of you feels excitement for being associated with something so wildly beautiful. The other part of you feels the shameful need to morph into something gentler to hide the wild part of your nature.

This woman was me eight years ago. I don't ask you to imagine her because I hope to find healing from reactions I cannot witness. Instead,

I want you to know that when I refer to a wild heart or a wild hearted woman, I am referring to the heart of every woman who's been told that she's too much as she is and there isn't a place for her unless she adopts a mold that was made for someone else but she is somehow expected to fit. As I speak to my past self in the words that fill these pages, I want you to know that I see *you* too and am speaking to you in all your wildness. I embrace the lessons that will lead you home to yourself as you follow the compass meant only for your wild heart to follow.

LESSON ONE: THE WORLDS OF THE HEART

Walking through the woods isn't much different than immersing yourself in the energy of your heart space. Both embody dynamic shades of green to let us know we are home within ourselves. Both facilitate the steady flow that circulates and sustains life. Both create steady, rhythmic sounds to remind us that even when we feel most lost, we are always safely held. Both reach beyond what our eyes see to whisper messages of love when our souls need it most. I often find myself wondering where one begins and where the other ends. These spaces carry similar energetic purposes but there are differences that keep us disconnected enough that we forget what it means to fluidly move from one space to the next.

Nature embodies many facets of our human hearts while also carrying a silent reassurance that is waiting to hold each of us when we remember to come home to her. Her seasons may change but the foundation of love, life, lessons learned, and inner knowing she carries remain the same. Nature is the compass to our hearts and to our center.

The heart recognizes the magic of the world within and around its protective shell. In turn, it asks not to hold more but to be held so it can be the most vital form of itself. The heart that beats within each of us is a steadfast constant that carries us through the purpose we are meant to live. Your heart is the key that unlocks the magic held in the spirit nature gives you.

The hard decision that each of us faces is whether we will allow ourselves to discover what it means to build the bridge that connects the heart of nature to the heart of our physical bodies; gifting us a vibrant, aligned connection to our purpose and ourselves. If we choose one over the other, we spend our lives attempting to simulate what we think could be our purpose. Regardless of where we are in this moment, there is an opportunity to hold or be held by the journey to healing the collective heart space, our heart opening moment.

LESSON TWO: UNDERSTANDING

My moment arrived while I was watching my horse, Pie, being tattooed in vibrant watercolor ink onto my arm. I remember wanting to keep his gentle, but wild energy with me as a reminder to embody this duality in my heart even when I felt disconnected with myself. I understand now that this was my heart's plea to let the full spectrum of its essence be seen by me and ultimately the world. The moment that I saw the rainbow of colors bringing the heartbeat of my horse's spirit to life I felt my own heart skip a beat. I knew then that this wasn't just a tattoo, it was a promise to myself to build my bridge, connect the worlds of the heart and embrace the magic that would unfold. As the next color, green, was being added to Pie's mane, I felt myself shake off the revelation that had just found me and suddenly shrink back into myself.

That's the funny thing about being human, isn't it? We recognize the comfort of known quantities. It's easier to operate in the familiarity of a predictable space than to step out of the shadows and courageously move toward the bigness of our dreams. In this space the pilot light of our heart is on but the flame that lights it is as faint as the ornate bridge that connects the worlds of the heart. I'd allowed myself to choose to remain unseen because I was scared to break free from the stories I'd been told about myself and nurture the impact I knew in my heart was mine to make. *I was hiding.*

I operated in this space for years as I waged a silent battle within my heart. The wounds I carried from traumas that changed the course of my life forever were complicated and deep. The stories that flew through my mind each day were the ones I'd been told by the men I loved through the early part of my adult life. They weren't stories that celebrated the spirit I held as a woman, rather they were stories that reminded me that my creativity made me unpredictable, my spontaneity made me untamable, and my quirkiness made me unlovable. I could no longer see myself when I looked in the mirror because after I'd heard the same stories enough times, I began to accept them as my truth. I stifled my creativity, I eliminated spontaneity and I did my best to be as normal as possible. I built a titanium wall around my heart and looked at the world with eyes that longed to soften at the simple, magical joy of hearing Pie's steady breathing as we galloped through open fields.

During my competitive years in the horse world, I knew exactly who I was, and that knowledge made me feel invincible. I had no fear when I climbed the mounting block to put my foot in the stirrup and less fear when I experienced the world heels down and reins in hand. There was such reassurance in the rhythmic sound of air moving through Pie's lungs and the beat of his hooves carrying me around each over fences course as the intuitive whispers of our hearts connected to travel the adventure of each new obstacle. All I needed to know was that my sixteen-year-old heart was connected to the heart of my horse, and the heart of the world around me. In this season of my life, I knew how to surrender to the voice of my intuition and to let it guide me. The rest fell into place.

LESSON THREE: SURRENDER

Each of us has a moment, often several carrying the same message, that alters us to the very core of our being. It usually isn't until the fourth or fifth message that our skin tingles with goosebumps, our mind begins to focus on what is being conveyed to us and most importantly what on Earth to do with it all. There isn't a neatly wrapped package we can open to learn how to take our next steps forward. Instead, the lesson we receive by making the active choice to reconnect to our heart is one of surrender. We can spend a lifetime ignoring the chatter of our internal compass to glide through life feeling a range of contentedness or we can surrender to the fear our mind interprets as it tries to make sense of the incoming paradigm shift. Surrender requires us to be willing to see the strength we carry within ourselves as well as our ability to discover the full spectrum of who we are by breaking the habit of who we think we're supposed to be, to be ourselves without confirmation.

The act of surrender feels liberating because it carries transformative energy. However, the recognition that we are living a life out of alignment with ourselves does not mean that we look only at the negative in our lives so there is a scapegoat to absorb rashly made life altering decisions. Surrender means that a deeply rooted inner knowing is allowed to surface to guide you to your heart's purpose as you release control of your expectations of the outcome.

I'd known for years that this season of my life would come. It was time for me to intentionally flip my world upside down so that I could be free to heal the connection between the worlds of the heart and lead myself home. I promised myself that day in the tattoo shop that if I took the bold steps into the unknown that awaited me, I would use the stories of my journey to heal the hearts of women just like me. Wild hearted women who knew there was more to themselves and that *more* was heartfelt medicine for the world. I couldn't live one more day feeling trapped within myself. I knew it was time to answer the persistent calls of my heart to walk through the woods and build my bridge so I could teach others how to do the same.

As I welcomed each new year and the rites of passages along the way, I slipped back into the silent battle with myself. I felt like I was doing all the things I was supposed to do, but I felt so far from the girl who experienced life with such a deep connection to the life around her. I wondered why my marriage felt empty, why I was often chided (even scolded) for thinking the way I did. Why I'd had to hear that I only had my job because I was pretty, why my right leg could no longer work with my left to run (an act I learned later was sacred to me because it mirrored the connection I needed with the heart of nature) and why I just couldn't stop crying. I was lost, vulnerable and absolutely cracked open. I was ready to surrender, and I finally understood why it was so important.

LESSON FOUR: CONNECTION

I wasn't a perfect wife or even a very good one in my first marriage so it's no surprise that my marriage felt empty. The relationships we build with the ones we love mirror back the relationship we maintain with ourselves. Clearly, I was below passing on both counts and it often baffled me because there should have been no glaring reason that we couldn't have been blissfully happy together, but we weren't. The decision to leave my marriage was the most difficult choice I've made in this life because it required that I allow myself to be seen as just me, which was terrifying after trying so hard to blend in and blindly accept the stories the world told me about myself. I knew that the story I carried in my heart wouldn't be understood for a long time, but I just knew it was my calling to redefine the piece of my life that was holding me back so that I could step onto my own stage and be the woman I was meant to be all along.

After years of searching for answers to heal my wounds I experienced invaluable mentorships, earned multiple holistic wellness certifications, and began coaching others on how mindfulness and nutrition could create profound healing. I was closer to building the bridge, but something was missing because I still felt like I was hiding behind the years of learning I'd claimed had healed the bridge between the worlds of the heart. In truth, I had grown more than I thought possible but the words I spoke to the first hearts I guided, sounded like the many voices that imparted their wisdom to me instead of my own voice sharing the message from my heart. I felt like an imposter.

The dialogue of healing what feels broken or lost within our hearts is never-ending, but it holds such potent medicine if we give it permission to continue. When we act without knowing the voice of our heart, the bridge we've worked so hard to build begins to fade away piece by piece. In this moment of fear that we've come so far for so little we have an opportunity to make an empowered choice to have the audacity to be ourselves without confirmation to unearth the true voice of our heart.

For me, I knew there was only one path left to take to fully connect with the whispers of my heart. I had to immerse myself in the heart of nature. I laugh a little as I read that last sentence because I didn't go camp out in the woods for a year to find myself. Instead, I walked down the hill behind the home I now share with the man I was always meant to find, to spend time by the creek, which I now affectionately call the Riverbank. Every day in this space I surrounded myself with the shades of green on the grass, weeds, wildflowers, and leaves. I closed my eyes to listen to the effortless flow of water over and around the rocks as it traveled past me. I opened my ears to hear the birds chirping, the cracks of each branch and the movement of the deer I knew were right across the water. I asked my heart to open to receive the affirmation that this was the medicine I needed. My skin tingled with goosebumps and my eyes shed tears that came not from sadness but from an overwhelming sense of knowing that I'd found my place. My bridge was rebuilding, and my lesson of connection was complete.

LESSON FIVE: HEARING THE WHISPERS OF YOUR HEART

I began to see the magic and the medicine in the moments where a fox would curl up across from me, content to share silent time together, where the pain in my leg would dissipate when my body was immersed in the cold water of the creek and the intangible guidance I received from the life taking place around me and for me. I understood that my disconnect from nature created the emptiness I held within myself. With each new experience I understood why the countless hours spent in the throes of learning all the things I craved, gave me knowledge of facts but not of myself. No one else could find the path to my heart or its purpose but me. Nature and all her intuition were always there waiting for me to arrive and claim my place by the Riverbank. Waiting for me to embrace each new experience as I remembered that there was no mold I could fit, other than the one I designed to expand with my growing consciousness.

The more time I spent connecting to the heart of nature and her whispers, the more the connection I rebuilt within myself spilled over to my community. I could feel the titanium wall around my heart melting away. New friendships blossomed and sisterhood wounds of the past healed. I witnessed myself walking through woods that used to feel so strange to me and now became the home within myself, where I could be as wildly creative as I needed and could simultaneously nurture my soul with gentleness. The path to my heart's purpose was clear. The lush green plants that once covered it, now parted so that it could guide each new sister that nature nudged towards me, in rebuilding her own bridge. So she could discover the world of hearts meant to hold and be held by her wild heart alone. Everywhere I looked, healing was happening. I wasn't hiding, *I was leading because I could hear the whispers in my heart.*

* * *

DEAR HEART-CENTERED LEADER,

You are gifted with freedom and creativity in this season of your life. Now is the time for you to fully engage in this vibrant, expansive energy to rekindle the fire within your heart.

Know that the obstacles that find you are there for you. They serve as the beacons to guide you out of the shadows and into the light only you can embody to share as medicine to the world.

Give yourself permission to let the wind rush through your hair and fill your lungs as your legs cross the bridge you've built to the worlds of the heart. Embrace the healing in lovingly releasing the wounds that are no longer yours to carry and feel the flame in your heart burn more brightly with each new step forward.

Remember that no matter where you go or what you decide to do, you will never be alone. You are seen, you are held, and you are the holder of your worlds of the heart.

I invite you now, Wild Heart, to explore where your walk in the woods ends and where your heart space begins. This is the walk of the heart-centered leader. May your adventure begin.

With loving wildness,

Katie Lee

KATIE FORSE

Katie Forse is an Intuitive Healer. She is the curator of the Intuitive Healing Shop and creator of the WHISPER healing method. Her mission is to show wild hearted women how to embrace life's ebb and flow to bring balanced fluidity to their journey of healing. She believes that when we connect with nature, energy and intuition; the whispers of healing flow with ease as we awaken to our most vibrant, aligned selves. Katie's WHISPER healing pedagogy calls upon seven animal archetypes to help us understand the energy we hold in our present and how to connect with the energy we need to balance our healing work. Her guidance leads us to the moments of synchronicity that serve as reminders of the many ways our healing can be claimed by the joy nature's whispers rekindle in our wild hearts.

Website: www.intuitivehealingshop.com

Instagram: @wildheartedintuitive

Email: hello@intuitivehealingshop.com

SIMULTANEOUS HEALING: TOGETHER WE WALK—AS WE LEARN, BECOME AWARE, AND EVOLVE

The mind boggled to some extent on how to express myself in this more casual format, compared to the academic style in which I am used to writing. I share with you my evolution into becoming a heart-centered, trauma-informed, trauma thriver, therapist. Expressing how this evolution came to be requires me to trace back to two decades ago when the childhood dream of becoming a psychotherapist started to come to fruition with my entering graduate school for my Masters Degree in Social Work. And also at that time, my own understanding of the psychological trauma that I had been exposed to moved from deep within the core of myself to a gradual recognition, awareness, and acceptance.

As I would learn, first academically and then personally, the process of healing from trauma is multifaceted and multi-layered. It can be analogous to the peeling of the layers of an onion in the sense that there are many areas of the self that are impacted by exposure to psychological trauma. Further, even though psychological trauma is a part of the human experience, there appears to be a ubiquitous denial and an avoidance of one having experienced trauma, rather than an acceptance of it. Sadly, in these cases, the root cause of the distress often goes undetected or misdiagnosed and the individual often experiences years of confusion and discomfort. It is my hope in this chapter to openly and vulnerably share my own experiences of psychological trauma that provided my path to knowledge, awareness, and evolution, and finally discuss how both are incorporated into a heart-centered approach to support the movement through psychological and emotional healing with my clients.

It's interesting that my writing process engendered a first draft that was analogous to those who have been exposed to trauma - avoidant, disconnected, and distant. As I contemplated for quite some time how to mentally and emotionally return to the writing of this chapter, I realized, with support, that maybe the best and only way to speak to the readers of this chapter is to share more deeply from my heart and soul about my own history of psychological trauma. As well as the ongoing nature of a posttraumatic stress response despite years of healing, and how I incorporate my own exposure to trauma with the work that I facilitate with my clients.

Many years ago as a young and eager social worker, I recall a supervisor stating boldly, but also in a somewhat nonchalant way that there was nothing like a shared experience. I knew what this supervisor was referring to, but I felt conflicted. In graduate school, we had been taught ad nauseum to be extremely judicious around any form of self disclosure, and that it should be done minimally or not at all. Although from an academic perspective, this made perfect sense to me, from a pragmatic, real world, perspective, it didn't. Back then, I followed the academic perspective for fear of "doing something wrong", a trauma response itself as I would come to later discover, and continued my work with clients with minimal disclosure. And at the time, that felt right. However, as I reflect back on that time now, I wonder if that too was an outcome of the traumatic exposures that I had experienced throughout my life.

As stated previously, psychological trauma is often understated in our society, and many mental health conditions are considered without a deeper exploration of what may be at the root of the condition—posttraumatic stress. It has been my experience both personal and professional that psychological trauma is an insidious beast that rears its ugly head during critical and pivotal times in life, during times of transition, as well as during times of stagnancy. Essentially, psychological trauma can present itself at any time, and I suppose that is my story as well. Throughout my life, I had experienced profound anxiety, both generalized and social, and I also experienced periods of depressed mood. I also recognized that I had some family of origin challenges, but I always thought to myself - who didn't? As an adult, I had come to accept that I was just an anxious person who occasionally had periods of sadness, and an occasionally challenging family of origin. Never at that time, had I considered myself an individual who had experienced psychological trauma, even though I had a plethora of education in Psychology and Social Work by then.

It wasn't until my early thirties during attendance at a professional development workshop on psychological trauma, that I had a profound paradigm shift in mindset both personally and professionally. If ever there was a moment in life where the puzzle pieces rapidly melded together, it was at this workshop as I attentively listened to the presenter. It was in those moments that I had the recognition that what was being discussed was exactly what I had experienced at various times during my life. I felt raw and vulnerable as I released years of pent up confusion and emotion at that training. I was also flabbergasted that as a Post-Masters professional in mental health, I had only associated psychological trauma with combat or severe abuse, rape, etc. How did it take over thirty years and numerous years of both mental health education and experience for me to finally self identify as an individual who had experienced numerous traumatic events throughout her life? It would be safe to say that that moment was also the genesis of my healing process from my own trauma. At the inception, my healing primarily consisted of self education - learning anything and everything that I could about psychological trauma and posttraumatic stress. It was definitely a time of self exploration and discovery, self acceptance and gentleness. Little did I know back then how far I would still have to go in order to begin to experience and feel some semblance of peace from my psychological trauma.

Parallel to this personal experience of healing, my career expanded and the focus of all of my work with clients was related to supporting individuals in working towards the healing process of their own trauma. Somehow in those early days and as my own self-understandings were crystalizing, I think I found strength and inspiration in those who were transforming as they received treatment for their own and various traumatic experiences. Their success, as well as ability to resolve their posttraumatic stress was incredible to me. They were doing what I couldn't at the time - facing their trauma rather than avoiding it.

As this process ensued, I began to further realize that there were so many aspects of myself, alive and active, that were merely the resultant of my unhealed, or rather, unaddressed psychological trauma. I was curious, and I suppose I was also avoidant—avoiding addressing my own trauma as I excelled as a professional who supported others in their healing. Why was I avoiding healing my own trauma or at least attempting to start to heal? What was I so afraid of? I would soon find out, as the unhealed trauma culminated in my life which ultimately led to the demise of my marriage.

It wasn't until I moved through my own divorce that I began to recognize the depths of my posttraumatic stress and complex PTSD. I began to understand how just merely existing as a traumatized individual had impacted my life in so many ways, and at the time I thought, quite possibly positioned me on the 'wrong' life trajectory. I began to recognize that I lived an experience where my central nervous system was likely activated more times than not, that the previous periods of depression and anxiety in my life were maybe more likely a symptom of my history of trauma rather than actual stand alone diagnoses. I began to learn and eventually understand that my trauma began during childhood, as it does for most of us. This statement is certainly not to issue blame towards my parents or to any adults who were present for me during my formative years. Learning and understanding our childhood traumas is important because it allows us to trace back and to gain increased perspective on who we are and of our life experiences. It allows us to recognize that our own caretakers were likely parenting from a place of unhealed trauma, and that recognition doesn't necessarily mean that we forgive and forget, but it allows us to gain this knowledge and move forward with compassion and love.

During this same time, I also recognized the importance of mindfulness and spirituality in the healing process. I had begun a daily meditation process that was extremely effective at supporting a feeling of calm and safety. I incorporated a better understanding of mindset and how my thoughts and words worked inside of my brain. It was a period of I think possibly re-birth and essentially learning how to be a human being and how to function in the world, or to at least try better than I had before.

I started seeing my life like an ocean wave, complete with absolutely wonderful memories and life experiences that I felt tremendously and profoundly grateful for. However, interspersed within those wonderful memories were always some traumatic memories or even continued traumatic experiences. Some were perceived as less profound and as I reflected back, others deeply impacted me and my perception on myself and the nature of the world as a whole. I remember spending the better part of young adulthood through my mid-thirties in a highly activated nervous system. By this time, I had a wonderful, consistent, and safe support person in my life who was calming and loving. I am thankful for this support because it was this that enabled me to, from a nervous system and trauma perspective pursue my education and my career to the fullest extent.

I contemplated major life decisions, major life mistakes and regrets. I vacillated back and forth between thinking what's wrong with me so I can overcome and gain mastery of this thing called trauma. For a number of years, I not only researched the most effective techniques and therapies for treating trauma, but I also experimented with them on myself. I understood the basic process that needed to unfold, and this was something that I learned back in my earlier years as a therapist when I first received my EMDR training. I knew that I needed to address all of the trauma that resided in the subconscious parts of my brain. Address them by re-visiting them in a controlled setting with a vertically integrated brain.

Not too long ago, I also reflected on what I had been taught many years ago, how there is nothing like a shared experience. I had remembered choosing what I deemed to be the 'safe' path back then when working with clients - not sharing - or perhaps I just didn't know enough to share back then. More recently, I have come to understand the importance of shared experience when working with clients, as well as offering disclosure about my own history of trauma and the subsequent and ongoing healing processes that have ensued in my life. It is understood in trauma therapy that the rapport that a client and therapist share with each other is one of the most important aspects of healing and growth. Recently, a client with an extensive history of trauma and a mental health professional also, shared with me how important it has been to them knowing that I too, have an extensive history of psychological trauma. They shared that knowing that I can fully understand the depth and complexities of the actual lived experience of what it is like to "have trauma' and work to heal from trauma has been both significant and transformative in their own healing process.

My self disclosure of my own psychological trauma begins online on my social media accounts, as well as my website. It continues, with care, wisdom, and clinical expertise in my work with clients through a treatment process that I have and continue to incorporate in my own healing.

As humans, we are connected and interconnected, and our energies are synchronous. What impacts you impacts me and vice versa. As I learn and grow and heal, you are affected by my healing. I am a case study of one, and my clients, friends, and those around me are able to benefit and experience the results of this anecdotal research. It's dichotomous to some extent - simple, yet complex, intense, yet freeing, deep, yet light and easy, scientific, yet spiritual, clinical, yet intuitive, unchanged, yet constantly evolving.

As it stands currently, the treatment used with clients is a multi-step process incorporating both science and the ideas of love and compassion in a cyclical way as a mechanism to support individuals in the forward progression towards continued and ongoing healing. The following list depicts the steps involved in this process: awareness and validation, education as a method to increase an individual's knowledge, incorporation of positive coping strategies, trauma processing, reparenting and renewal, reflect and repeat as necessary. What follows is a brief description of each step in the treatment process.

Awareness and Validation: Developed in the aforementioned text of this chapter, it is often that individuals present in the therapeutic setting with an array of concerns, ranging from various self-diagnoses, dysregulated emotions, activated nervous systems, and most commonly, challenges in navigating relationships with others. Many clients simply do not recognize that all of these components equate to a history of trauma, generally complex trauma. Supporting clients on just the awareness that what they are describing to me is trauma, is an extremely validating and breakthrough experience for clients. Many receive this awareness and validation as a relief, similar to the lifting of a heavy weight. Awareness and validation offer the client an answer for what has ailed them for years - they are vital components in the beginning phases of trauma treatment.

Education and Knowledge Attainment: The next step relates to offering education for the purposes of the individual acquiring knowledge about themselves. Knowledge is power, and knowing about the self is transformative. Addressed from a neuroscientific perspective, I share the research and teachings of those formative trauma researchers who so inspired me as I began to develop my own knowledge on psychological trauma. Knowing the inner mechanisms of the brain, knowing exactly what is happening as one's nervous system becomes activated and emotions move into dysregulation is a powerful tool, empowering to the self, and a gift of love to the recipient.

Positive Coping Strategies: Typically, individuals who have a history of psychological trauma incorporate any strategy positive or negative, that will help to alleviate the dysregulation that is felt throughout the self and the body. Part of the therapeutic work is to support individuals in integrating positive coping strategies into their repertoire. One primary positive coping strategy that I offer to clients is the opportunity to learn and develop a meditation and mindfulness practice. It is my belief that mindfulness is imperative to the trauma healing process in that engaging in these coping strategies supports neuroplasticity and also leads to an individual becoming the observer to their lived experiences, rather than identifying as these experiences.

Trauma Processing: Accessing the traumatic information where it resides is crucial to the healing process. Because the traumatic information is haphazardly arranged in the subconscious areas of the brain, just talking about the trauma and working to incorporate coping strategies alone is simply not enough to create the shift necessary in order to stimulate the healing process. Although talking and strategizing methods for navigating through life with trauma triggers can be helpful from a knowledge-building perspective, when an individual actually does experience a trigger, the part of the brain that is responsible for activating and remembering what strategies to implement, goes offline, thereby rendering the strategies useless in the moment of most need. Eye Movement Desensitization and Reprocessing (EMDR) incorporates bilateral stimulation of the brain (generally using alternating lights) as a mechanism for accessing the subconscious brain, identifying the traumatic information, moving the traumatic information, and ultimately enabling the individual to have a different perception of self, self in relation to others, and self in relation to the world.

Reparenting and Renewal: Being able to care for the self emotionally, and have confidence in one's ability to provide safety, love, nurturance, and security to the self is another critical and powerful shift on the healing journey. As an individual begins to process their trauma experiences, they become more capable of caring for themselves. Reparenting the self is vital to support individuals in the perceptual shifts related to the trauma processing.

Reflect and Repeat: Similar to peeling the layers of an onion, healing trauma can be just that, and as each layer is peeled away, deep reflection and observation of the next steps becomes an important part of this process.

One part of healing trauma is recognizing that you have the power to change the trajectory of your life and the power to change how you exist in this world. Another part is recognizing that we are on this journey together. All those years ago when my mentor haphazardly shared this crucial advice, "There's nothing like a shared experience," I wasn't quite ready to hear it. Sometimes learning to lead requires a process of unlearning how you were told to do so. I believe we're always being led deeper into our truest and best selves, sometimes it looks like rewriting a chapter for a book, sometimes it looks like a client inspiring you with their resilience, and sometimes it's a mentor casually saying one short sentence that changes your life. Regardless of how your life unfolds, as humans, we are never intended to "go it alone." Our connection to one another and our commitment to our own betterment is what catalyzes our growth and directs us toward the greatest medicine of all… our humanity.

TARA THERESE BULIN, PH.D, LCSW-R

Tara Bulin, Ph.D. LCSW-R is a Doctor of Social Work and a Licensed Clinical Social Worker with an expertise in psychological trauma. She has extensive clinical, hospital-based administration, outpatient agency experience, and has dedicated several years serving as an adjunct professor. Dr. Bulin is trained in Eye Movement Desensitization and Reprocessing (EMDR), and she integrates this therapeutic approach quite regularly with individuals she works with who have been exposed to trauma and posttraumatic stress.

Additionally and complementary in her practice with clients, Dr. Bulin has certification in teaching mindfulness techniques and meditation. She strongly believes that the treatment of psychological trauma must be two-fold, incorporating clinical aspects of psychology and neuroscience, as well as spirituality, in a comprehensive and meaningful way in order to offer healing of the individual from a mind, body, and soul perspective.

Website: www.taratherese.com

Instagram: @dr.taratherese

WHY YOU NEED A QUARTER LIFE CRISIS

"You are either going to get this out of your system or it's going to change you forever."

I swallowed as my eyes made their way past the bowl of steaming spaghetti and meat sauce as I looked up to meet my mom's eyes. I had just ridden my bicycle 51 miles from the East Village in Manhattan to my parents house in Stamford, CT, and was currently fueling up to ride 49 more miles back into New York City that same afternoon.

"Hmp," I nodded in wonderment with a closed lip smirk.

* * *

HERE I SIT SLOUCHED in my cushioned chair boxed in by the five-foot tall walls of my three sided cubicle in lower Manhattan. I find myself holding a far off stare at a stack of manila folders on my desk. More change orders. The folders resemble pancakes, and my boss Michael, an IHOP waiter is endlessly piling on pancake after pancake forcing me to have another bite after I already had five bites too many. Enough to make you want to throw up.

Michael calls my name from his corner office and shakes me out of my reverie. It's these visits to his office where I get a glimpse of the Freedom Tower. One World Trade Center. Our project. I am reminded that this is the dream job for any twenty-five-year-old civil engineer. To work on a building that symbolizes the resilience and fortitude of this country. A statement to the terrorist who took down the Twin Towers that we will not be intimidated.

Yet working on this project doesn't please me at all. There is no excitement about the work I am doing. In fact, it only frightens me further. If this won't make me happy, what will?

Happiness.

Isn't *this* happiness? Shouldn't I be happy?

I did what I was supposed to do. I graduated college and became a civil engineer in the 'greatest city in the world.' Now I get to spend the next forty years, Monday through Friday, 8am to 5pm with only two weeks of vacation building giant skyscrapers in an overcrowded city to create more space for more people to help build someone else's dream.

I gulped. Fear set in. That same question now became a taunt. 'Shouldn't I be happy?'

But I'm not.

I saw the next forty years already chosen for me. I move in with my girlfriend of three years, we get married, we have babies, we move to the suburbs, our kids go to college while I continue to force down more pancakes. But at least I'll be in the corner office, right?

"No!" my entire body screamed. "No, no, this can't be it!" So one day I had a thought. Actually, it was a declaration.

"I am going to ride my bicycle across America!"

I don't know if this will solve anything but I know I have to do something. Something *I* deem remarkable. Not a path chosen for me. Not happiness defined by someone else. Happiness defined by me. Is a bike trip across America happiness? How should I know? But I know what I'm doing right now isn't.

* * *

A DEEP TREPIDATION swept over me as the sea filled rain smacked my lips. I turned south toward Seaside, Oregon and could hear the sounds of the ocean waves crash down as if begging me to stay away. "Don't end this journey" they urged as they beat the shoreline.

My dread was overcome by pure joy and adrenaline knowing I was about to see my family for the first time in ninety days. In less than 20 miles we would celebrate the capstone of my bike ride across America by dipping my front wheel in the Pacific Ocean.

"LOOOOOVE! REIGN O'ER ME!" I sang on SnapChat with enthusiasm. Not a single thing could break my stride now!

I leaned into my final right turn of the trip and heard my family before I could make them out. My dad was the loudest, screaming "WooWOO!!" which had become my signature holler throughout my trip as I descended each magical hill. Now this time my family was here to experience the magic with me in my final feet of these 5,019 miles.

I envisioned this heroic final moment many times on this trip. The same way I would imagine hitting a walk off grand slam for the New York Mets as a young boy in the backyard of our Connecticut home. Our dreams keep us going. They keep us motivated and disciplined about pursuing a future that seems silly or impossible to everyone else, but in utter alignment with your deeper knowing.

However, unlike stomping on home plate surrounded by your teammates, I found myself stomping on wet pavement surrounded by the people I love most, my family. We poured champagne, hugged, told stories of the summer, but that earlier trepidation continued to lay heavy on my mind.

So now I go back to New York City to be a civil engineer?

This thought plagued my mind as I spent the next week with my family traveling the coast of California. I just had the best ninety days of my life. Sure, some days were hard, scary, and even moments when I wanted to quit, but I also learned what it meant to be present which transformed those hardships into truly joyous moments. I would never have had that perspective in New York.

So, I just rode my bike across America. I thought. I did something for myself for the first time in my life. That's something a lot of people never do. *I know my life can be filled with daily happiness. I just saw it for ninety straight days.* That's when it clicked. Life truly is the journey, not the destination.

Most of our lives are spent chasing the next best thing. We get to spend a brief moment in time where we spray champagne and celebrate our accomplishments with the ones we love and then we are onto chasing the next thing.

If 99.9% of our lives consist of the pursuit of the next best thing, what would our lives be like if we learned to *love* the pursuit? Not to bear through our toughest times, but to fall in love with them. If we truly get one chance at life, what if we find that we get to experience the hard times for our benefit? We get to feel scared and do things anyway because we know on the other side of fear is the person we so badly want to be? What if we get to unapologetically pursue what lights us up because when we lay on our deathbed looking up at the ones we love we get to say, "I gave it everything I had. I stopped giving into the fear and the judgment of others because they don't know my truth. Only I do and I lived a life full of the things that piqued my curiosity and ignited my soul. I have no regrets!"

As I sat in the front seat of the rental car, I smiled. Internally I made a new declaration, *I am on the pursuit of daily happiness.*

* * *

I WAS BACK in New York City and was grateful to have my previous employer take me back. Despite it being the winter of 2016, I rode my bike to work blasting through slush and biting wind and shrugging off the 22 mile round trip in 10 degree weather because being on my bike was my happy place.

Despite my gratitude, work was still uninspiring. That winter I applied to one of the best construction companies in the world. I got accepted and in one moment I was excited about the opportunity to be a part of the best in the world and in the next, I feared I was back to where I started back in 2015. Sure, I'm at a better company with greater room for growth, but is this the growth I am seeking?

I jumped back into the mold of the world around me. A world that rewards you for a prestigious career with an important job title and a salary to match. You remember, right? *Happiness.*

I was now driving the figurative Lamborghini. An amazing career with a world-class company that so many people would envy... but on the inside I was driving the Lambo with my foot slammed down on the brakes. A deeper part of me refused to lose sight of my desire for daily happiness. Still without a clear understanding of what that meant, I pushed myself to begin pursuing more things that lit me up, just as I did with cycling.

I joined my old college friend's flag football team in Hoboken, New Jersey. We went on to win the championship. I pulled out an old DSLR camera hidden away in my closet and fell in love with New York all over again as I spent hours after work photographing the city. I even discarded my preconceived notions about CrossFit and signed up for a free week. It was there that I found myself drenched in purpose.

I got home from work peeling the sweaty button down off my back. I checked Facebook and saw the owner of the CrossFit gym post on our private Facebook group.

June 10th, 2017

If there are any members who love CrossFit and have a desire to become a coach, we encourage you to get your CrossFit certification and we will mentor you to become a coach!

I sat there reading this message as butterflies of excitement tickled my stomach.

I was thrown back to 2008. A freshman in college studying business and not having the college experience I saw in the movies. I struggled to make a ton of friends and I was not hooking up with girls left and right. It was the gym that became my escape from expectations built on false fantasies. One Friday evening as I re-racked my dumbbells I thought, "I would love to be a personal trainer, but that's not a career path."

Back in my apartment in Brooklyn, a smile crept on my face.

Once again I realized how many decisions in my life have been based on someone else's idea of success or happiness. Of course the people closest to me have only ever wanted the best for me, but how could anyone possibly know what is best for me?

It became obvious that I knew exactly what I wanted nine years ago and in an instant I talked myself out of it because of the lessons I was taught growing up. Naively I believed all of those lessons as truths and they unconsciously shaped my journey.

Our beliefs about the world become engrained through heightened emotion and repetition by the authorities in our life throughout our life. The pesky thing about beliefs is that we stop questioning them because we take them for the truth, but only something that is true 100% of the time can be stated as truth. Everything else is just a belief that is meant to be shattered.

I grew up in the Connecticut suburbs. It was never in question that I would get a corporate job and move to New York City. This story of success and happiness began to shatter around me. I could feel my soul expanding beyond this giant city and in my core I knew, it was time to leave.

* * *

THE PLAN WAS SIMPLE. I have been working out since I was fourteen-years-old; I have helped friends and family; I got my certification and have been a part time CrossFit coach and personal trainer for the past year. I will plant firm roots in Denver and continue being an engineer for one year and then I would go all in on my passion for fitness.

Despite my working on prestigious projects and my new company having a headquarters in Denver, I could not find a job. Not only that, I couldn't land an interview anywhere. With two months to go I still had zero leads on a job.

I leaned back in my chair, grabbed my phone and dialed my boss.

"HR says the Denver office isn't accepting any transfers. Is there nothing that can be done?" I asked.

"I'm sorry, I've put in my recommendation and spoke to the managers there, but there's no work." I sighed, thanked her and hung up.

I pulled myself out of my seat and walked a few blocks to pier 96 overlooking the Hudson River. It was two years ago when I crossed this river on a ferry for Day 1 of my bike ride across America. *The best summer of my life was the summer I wasn't an engineer. I reflected. Being an engineer isn't my place in the world.* I smiled and turned my face up toward the sun, *Alright universe, I read you loud and clear. Fuck engineering. I'm going all in on personal training!*

* * *

I STOOD outside The Meatball Shop in Williamsburg, Brooklyn shuffling my feet back and forth and taking deep breaths to steady my nerves. It is one week before the big move to Colorado and I am meeting my dad for dinner, just us two.

I still hadn't told my dad about my decision to quit engineering. In fact, he was the only one I hadn't told. I knew how proud he was of the work I had put in and the incredible projects I'd worked on. I knew how much it meant to him to tell everyone that his son was a civil engineer in New York City. Most of all, I knew the sacrifices he had made, not just to put me through college, but to give me a life full of rich opportunities even before I was born.

I saw his Green Bay Packer hat and rosy cheeks as he ascended the subway stairs of the L train.

"Mugga Magoo!" he called. Only he called me Mugga. We hugged and he asked if I was ready to eat.

"Actually, I need to tell you something." I said as I stared down at the damp gray sidewalk spotted with centuries of old gum as I tried to remember how I scripted this in my head.

If I had the guts to look up at him at this moment, I may have seen him smiling, but I was afraid. I was afraid he would be disappointed that I am giving up five years of work in the field and four years of college for a silly hobby. I was afraid that he wouldn't understand my need to pursue a meaningful life in this way. I was afraid of not getting his approval which had meant so much to me throughout my life.

"Dad," it came out as a plea more than an addressment. "I know what it takes to be a really good engineer and I go to work and I don't want to do those things. But I know what it takes to be a really good personal trainer, and I'll do whatever it takes." I paused, but I couldn't back out now. With my eyes still lowered, my throat feeling constricted by the weight of the world, I finished, "When I move to

Colorado, I am not going to continue being an engineer. I am going to pursue my passion and be a full time personal trainer."

I clenched my jaw and looked up at him. His smile radiated pure love and understanding as he replied, "I know and you're going to do great."

Relief swept over me and pure bliss filled my heart as he pulled me in for a hug. We stood there embracing our unconditional love for each other before we made our way into the restaurant.

* * *

I KNOW YOU. You're like me. You want more out of life. You are a heart centered human looking to expand and change the world. You are here looking for clues on how to begin this process or maybe even expand your current leadership role.

While this book will give you many valuable tools and questions to ponder, you will never know what true leadership means if you don't first lead yourself. Einstein famously said, "You cannot solve a problem from the same level of consciousness that created it." In order to create a new level of consciousness you must take action, but not just any action. You must follow your heart and pursue what piques your curiosity!

I have been an engineer...

… a cyclist

… a personal trainer

… a photographer

… a brand expert

Here I sit today as a leadership, life and business coach.

I have hired coaches and I've done what people who loved me most told me to do and it still left me unhappy and unfulfilled.

Should you ride your bike across America? Maybe.

Should you quit your corporate job and move to Colorado to pursue your passion? How should I know?

What I do know is that there are no rules to this game of life. I wouldn't be the leader I am today and changing lives the way I am if I didn't cut out the noise and do what felt right to me down to my core. I didn't question it, I didn't wonder what my college buddies would think of me, and I definitely didn't wait for permission.

Just as my mom knew all along. There was no "getting it out of my system." The bike trip fundamentally changed who I am today. A spark was lit for me and I followed it. A spark has now been lit for you. Something came up for you while reading this chapter. *That's* the answer you've been looking for.

Stop waiting for permission. Stop looking at what everyone else is doing. Only you know the next right move. So go forward and lead from your heart.

MATTHEW ALLYN MICHALEK

Matthew Allyn is the founder of Powerful Leader Mastery and host of the Powerful Online Leadership podcast. If you are reading this then you have transformed your life and now you want to change the world by teaching others how to experience the same transformation as you. Matt's mission is to help coaches step into their power, learn how to become world-class coaches and market themselves as leaders in their industry.

Matt is driven by the deep desire to support people to take action toward their wildest dreams so when they are at the end of their life they will be confident they gave everything they had to this one precious life.

Matt currently lives in Colorado and loves playing baseball, trail running and snowboarding.

Website: www.matthewallyn.me

Instagram: @matthew.allyn

Podcast: Powerful Online Leadership

THE UNPAVED PATH

I took three deep breaths, wiped my tears, and walked up the stairs through the ambulance bay and into the ER. This had become an all too normal part of my routine. I created a habit out of making sure that I showed up to my night shift thirty minutes early so that I had enough time to cry and give myself the pep talk I needed in order to get myself through the door.

Every night I would contemplate how I could get out of it, and every night I would walk myself through those doors hoping that no one would notice the glassiness in my eyes, praying they couldn't sense how defeated I felt, or how badly I wished I didn't have to be there. Most of the time I did a pretty good job of shoving it down. I'd been suppressing the emotions just enough to get through my shift, focus on my patients, and pretend that everything was okay. But something about this night felt different.

I was assigned to critical care—where the sickest, most emergent, most likely to be teetering the line of death patients were placed. The patient board was completely full, every room was doubled, there were patients lining the hallway, and ambulance after ambulance continued to arrive.

All of a sudden it felt like the fluorescent lights and heat in the department had been turned up ten notches. Every single noise echoed as an overwhelming shrill through my entire body. My hands went numb and my head started spinning.

"Holy shit, I can't do this." I thought over and over and over again.

My face started tingling and I couldn't focus on anything because all of my senses were hyper focused on everything all at once.

"You have rooms 18-22."

"Are you ready to take report?"

"The lady in 19 just coded, we got her back, but it could happen again any minute."

"The gentleman in 20 is bleeding internally and needs a blood transfusion but the blood hasn't arrived yet."

"And you just got a new patient in room 22 who is having a lot of difficulty breathing, will probably need to be intubated, but we haven't been able to get respiratory support on the phone."

Suddenly the entire room went completely silent, I could no longer track the words that were coming out of her mouth, and the only thing I could hear was my own heart racing.

I'd been dealing with anxiety over work for a year and a half, which is how long it had been since I started the job, but I had never experienced anything like this before. My only thought processes were cycling around how desperately I needed to get myself out of this moment. How badly I needed to go home. How difficult it felt to breathe. And how weak I felt for my anxiety being the reason why I couldn't stick through this shift the same way I had been able to stick out every shift for the last year and a half.

"I feel like I'm going to throw up, I'm sorry, I'll be right back." I managed to get out.

I walked straight to the office, told my boss I was sorry but I had just received news of a family emergency and I was going to have to leave. I don't even think I waited for a response. I didn't even have the guts to talk about what was actually going on because it felt inexcusable. I felt like I was single handedly failing at the career I had spent seven years working to get. I had no backup plan, thousands of dollars in loans, no other options, no way out. Or at least that's what I told myself during that pre-shift pep talk for the next three years.

That was the moment it all started to fall apart, or in hindsight come together for me. The moment I finally admitted to myself that the career I had worked so hard, invested so much time, and so much money into, was not at all what I thought it was going to be. The moment I started to realize that I had done everything I was 'supposed' to do. I fit myself into every single box ever placed in front of me and truly believed in the success I was promised after doing so. I got good grades, got into a good college, took out the loans, studied my ass off, graduated with honors, passed my boards with ease, got the first job I ever applied for and was actually really really good at it. And yet somehow, I still felt like I was failing, and so was my belief in western medicine being a system that I wanted to be any part of.

Does this feel familiar to you? Unfortunately, I've come to believe that it's entirely too common for people today to be spending all of their time in exchange for money doing things they'd really rather not be doing - and that through continuing to do so they are perpetually living a life that is completely out of alignment with their true purpose and potential.

Although I realized relatively early on that this career was completely out of alignment with how I thought I would be helping people heal, I spent four and a half years watching the sick get sicker. I spent four and half years in an anxious state of hating my job, unable to help people truly heal the way my soul desired, and feeling like there was no way out. I watched patients revolve in and out of the hospital as if it were just a normal routine, as if it was the only option. It was as if they were completely incapable of learning another way. They had become so dependent on and defined by the chronic diseases they were diagnosed with, that they were taught to believe that it simply had to be who they were for the rest of forever. And who was I to blame them, I was doing the exact same thing. Simply accepting whatever was told to me as truth and giving away all of my power to perceive that there could ever be any other way.

I didn't think this deeply into it all at the time because, anxiety aside, I was a really good nurse. I fought hard for my patients, I desperately desired to give them the hope they had so clearly lost even while all the hope in my own life was slowly fading away. I was focused on how I could make the inevitable sadness of their lives a little bit brighter and I desired to be the light in their darkest moments. I wanted to ease their pain and suffering, make them smile, and make sure that they knew that they were being seen and heard as long as I was their nurse. My natural ability to continuously care as much as I did for my patients was the only reason I hung on for as long as I did.

It was exhausting. I was assigned eight patients at a time and I was expected to keep track of eight emergencies, show up for each of their needs, keep their pain under control, keep track of all of their lab tests and radiology screenings, make sure they were fed, warm, dry, and satisfied with the work I was doing.

They were never satisfied though. Nothing ever happened fast enough and no matter what, it was always the nurses fault. It was frowned upon to ever mention how many people we had to care for or to admit that we were spread so thinly that we were just trying to keep it all together. Truth was, every night I was in that ER, I was falling apart at the seams. I was simply trying to survive and make sure all of my patients did the same. I never felt like I had enough time, enough resources, enough eyes, arms, or legs to do the job that was being asked of me the way I had dreamed of doing it when I set out to become a nurse.

So many of the nurses and doctors I worked with were so burnt out, completely broken even. The longer I stayed, the more obvious it became that the humans that had high hopes when they set out to enter this field, would end up so jaded and frustrated with the level of human brokenness in these patients. So jaded that they would forget why they even got started in the first place. So many lost all of their empathy.

Fortunately, or maybe unfortunately, that was never the case for me. All I had was empathy. I cared so much about every single patient I came into contact with and it hurt me so deeply that I could hardly ever give them the time, attention, and deep human connection they desperately needed. I became a nurse to help people heal, and the inability to truly do so broke me. It became all too obvious to me that this system that I thought was built to help humans heal, was really just keeping them sick, stuck, and dependent on pharmaceuticals. And the system I had entered, with so much hope and pride in making a positive impact on the world, left me feeling sick, stuck, and grossly under appreciated.

The career I had worked so hard for was completely out of alignment with how I wanted to be serving the world. I could feel it in my soul that I wasn't helping people heal. I was another number in a system that began to feel like it was built to keep people stuck. And that system was working, because I was stuck, my patients were stuck, and none of us could see that there was any way out of the hands we'd been dealt.

I used to carry this idea in my head that the happiest, healthiest, most successful, and wealthiest people in the world were born winners. I thought that they simply had what it took to live the luxurious life of their dreams with effortless ease, and that I was not, nor would I ever be one of them. Little did I know then, that my biggest failure is where my self led and heart centered success started. The depression, anxiety, and panic attacks that ensued over the course of the 4 and a half years I spent as an emergency room nurse led my soul to search for a solution. For myself and unknowingly at the time, for the people I would go on to lead through their own holistic healing journey.

I found the first feelings of ease through a consistent yoga practice that slowly made my nursing shifts begin to feel a bit more bearable. I had practiced in the past, and always enjoyed the random one off classes I would go to, but it never stuck like this before. I was finding myself craving the feeling of lying on my back at the end of a class in a state of complete internal and external stillness. I quickly realized that it was a sensation I hadn't felt for as long as I could remember. How was it humanly possible that I had completely forgotten what it felt like to be at peace?

I was hooked. The more stillness I surrendered too, the more space I created that allowed me to listen to my soul. I went from going to classes a few times a week, to practicing every day, to finding myself on my mat multiple times a day. I had found a sanctuary within myself and my healing journey began.

One day a soul nudge whispered "get certified". At this point I was more used to fighting with my intuition than listening to it, but for whatever reason, it all fell into place perfectly, and I followed that nudge. I signed up for an immersive ten day yoga teacher training on Fire Island in New York and set out on a journey that I had no idea was about to change the entire trajectory of my life.

While I had gotten somewhat of a handle on it by then, my anxiety was still bad enough that I made my husband promise he would come and pick me up the next day if I felt like I needed him to, he told me I had to stick it out for at least three. But the second I stepped off the ferry, and into the little pink beach house that would create the space for the beginning of the greatest adventure of my life, I knew I was on my way home.

I knew there was something to yoga, a deeper reason as to why I felt such a sense of bliss every time I stepped on my mat, and I had heard teachers allude to the deeper philosophical teachings, but I had no idea the true healing power it held, and the journey it would take me on.

That week and a half turned a key in the center of my soul that unlocked a depth of healing I didn't know I needed and I had no idea existed. Slowly but surely the voice of my soul started to become familiar to me, and I continued to listen.

I went on to become 500 hour certified, to enroll in and complete a holistic nurse coaching course, to start a business making meditation beads, that turned into a business of building soul aligned programs created to help people move through their own internal healing journey. I found a mission, I found a passion, I found a purpose and I found the avenue through which I was going to be able to help people truly heal. When I woke up on the paved path that I'd previously been given and realized it didn't feel good to my soul, I stepped off that path, into the unknown, and forged my own.

Sometimes I waste time wishing I had known then what I know now. I wish that there had been someone in my corner letting me know that every struggle was for a greater purpose and every 'failure' was the exact lesson that my soul needed to learn on the path to success. So it's my hope, that as you read this, and through all of the work that I ever do that I get to be that person. That you get to see yourself, and feel your own struggles within my story. That you recognize within yourself the power I pulled out from within me to ditch the societal standards and expectations in exchange for the space and freedom to create life the way I desired to be living it.

The hard earned truth that I've come to understand is that winning takes a lot of losing. Success means being willing to fail. It means looking your fears in the face and making the firm decision that they will no longer stand in your way. It means jumping before you're ready and being willing to accept that those perceived failures are the exact lessons you need to learn in order to achieve your inevitable success. And while that perfectly planned destination seems shiny and sexy (believe me I thought that nursing career was the shiniest, and sexiest destination I would ever reach before I arrived) it's in the experiencing, the accepting, and the surrendering to the entire spectrum of the emotional journey that the true magic lies.

We are not nor have we ever been here to be a number in a system. To clock in, clock out, pay our bills, and hope that one day we happen to save enough to retire and then begin living our lives when they are three quarters of the way through. We are not here to stress so hard that we forget how to take care of ourselves and end up another patient in the system dependent on doctors appointments and prescription pills because we never learned how our minds, bodies, and spirits are meant to be cared for. That's never ever ever felt good to me and I assume, if you're reading this book that it's never felt quite right to you either.

So I guess my main message here is that you have the power. You have the power to create the life of your dreams. You have the innate ability to meet your mind, to heal your body, to face your fears, and to let go of any of the stories, stigmas, and beliefs that are stopping you from being, doing, and creating everything that is meant for your soul in this life's journey.

Your deepest fears can uncover your deepest desires. And your deepest desires are your soul's given blueprint to live out a limitless and extraordinary life of abundance and ease. It's all within you, it's always been within you, it's just been buried under the false truths we've been fed that we have to follow the paved path that was put in front of us in order to achieve success.

From this point forward you get to decide what success means to you. And the most sure fire way to walk that unpaved path to the true success your soul is ready to remember, is to tune in and listen. Follow the nudges, follow your joy, follow your desires—they are there, imprinted within you for a reason. And the sooner you learn to tap in and listen, the sooner you will begin leading your own heart centered journey to co-creating the life you were destined to live.

MOLLY ROSE RASANEN

Molly Rose Rasanen is the CEO of I'mperfectly Aligned, a registered nurse, transformational coach, and 500 hour trained yoga teacher. She helps high achieving women deepen their mind-body- spirit connection to achieve more success with less stress. Molly specializes in teaching the science and health benefits of spiritual practices and offers her clients the tangible tools to guide their inner healing and develop an individualized connection to their spirituality. As a travel ER nurse, Molly witnessed her patients falling through the cracks in western medicine. She saw that all illness was deeply rooted in humans being completely disconnected from their being. This sparked her deep dive into spirituality and alternative healing modalities. She believes in the power of the Mind and Body to heal itself and is passionate about being a part of the progress towards an integration of eastern and western practices in modern health care.

Instagram: @Mollyrasanen

Website: www.imperfectly-aligned.com

REDESIGNING LEADERSHIP

*I*f I could give my eighteen year-old self one piece of advice it would be to stop caring so much what others think and start focusing on what you believe about yourself. Ironically, it's the same advice I would give someone stepping into leadership.

I say this because I lived most of my life from a place of fear. Fear of making the 'wrong' choice and fear of the opinions of others. Fear of not leading in a way that others respected. What I've actually found is that letting go of fear will increase your success and effectiveness in leadership.

Not only was living in fear a destructive mindset, but I was exhausted by trying to be someone I'm not. The inauthenticity was actually creating more friction in myself. You see, your relationship with yourself is the most important relationship you will ever have. True success is liking yourself, liking what you do and liking how you do it. Without this it's going to be difficult to build trust, connection and feel fulfillment, let alone consider having an impact as a leader.

My hope in writing this and sharing my story is that you will be inspired and empowered to show up as the authentic leader you were meant to be by redefining leadership for yourself, your community and the impact you want to have on the world.

YOU DON'T KNOW WHAT YOU DON'T KNOW

Some of the best advice I ever received was in my mid-twenties by a fitness client who recently retired after decades of working in international business affairs. I called him after hitting a breaking point while working as a college Strength & Conditioning Coach at Clemson University. I really loved what I did, well let's be honest I loved aspects of what I did. The truth is college athletics is not nearly as glamorous as it sounds. I was feeling out of alignment with myself and the greater vision I had for my life. I also was putting undue pressure on myself to "figure out my life" and live up to the expectations of others. It was complex in that I was really good at being a coach and yet still something was missing.

After sharing the context of my situation (and hoping he would give me the perfect solution) he simply said, "You know Taylor I think this is really great that you know deeply this job isn't for you, because sometimes figuring out what you don't want is just as important as what you do want."

Let's just say in that moment this was not the advice I wanted to hear. I kind of brushed off the whole conversation after we hung up and felt frustrated. Meanwhile five years later I'm still talking about the impact this quote had on my life.

It took a while to realize that not only what he said was true, but sometimes figuring out WHO you don't want to be is just as important as figuring out who you do want to be. Which is really where my journey in leadership began. I was 27 years old when I decided to walk away from college athletics, which included turning down job offers at Texas A&M and University of Maryland. I wanted more out of my life and the idea of moving into the unknown was scary, exciting and a little bit daunting. This journey became the catalyst of creating my dream life and stepping into the Leader I was always meant to be.

MY COACHING START

I started my journey as a Psychology major at the College of Charleston, having no idea how the hell I was supposed to know what I wanted to do with my life at eighteen. Yet it was required to declare a major before stepping foot on campus. The only thing I knew was that I wanted to help people, so Psychology became the logical choice. However, I didn't make it past the first semester of school before switching my major to Exercise Science. I had recently learned that a friend I grew up playing baseball with had just started a job as a Strength & Conditioning Coach for the Minnesota Twins minor league baseball team. After talking on the phone with him, I instantly could feel that this was the dream job I didn't know existed.

This was one of the first times I really leaned into trusting my gut without letting thoughts or opinions from others come in. Without the fear of what others would think or say. While it was an unconventional career path, it felt so right to follow. This was a new but enlightening feeling for me, listening to the physical sensation in my gut. Later I would learn how important following this feeling would be to my success. I'm confident you have this knowing and instinct too; you may just have not created the awareness to follow it fully.

When I chose to pursue a career in college strength & conditioning it was never on my radar the lessons I would learn around leadership, personal development and improving the quality of your life. An important lesson here is that you will never know how the path you are on will lead to your long-term destination. Twenty-year-old, Taylor would have laughed if you told him one day, he would become a Life and Leadership Coach. You'll never know what lessons you will find in the most unorthodox of places. I'm going to share with you a few examples, both of which shaped my current role as a leader and coach.

THE GOOD, THE BAD & THE UGLY

I want to preface that I learned a lot of amazing qualities from some of the best coaches and athletes in the world. I am grateful for the opportunities, experience and impact all of the people I've worked with have had on me. What I'm going to share is only part of the story. However, it is an important part because what stuck with me was a lot of what doesn't work or felt unauthentic. Seeing these things started my practice of curiosity to ask: "is there a better way?"

In the college setting there is a lot of politics and pressure to win. There is rarely enough time to slow cook the process of creating connections and foundation to build a winning culture. Especially considering there are new athletes coming in and out every year. The expectation is to win yesterday, and with that urgency I've seen many coaches take on a leadership style of 'force'.

I believe that leading through force arose as a defense mechanism from a place of survival. When things don't go as planned it's easy for confidence to be shaken, ensuing in a leadership style that demands one to "do as I say" and "get in line". I saw some of the most intelligent coaches fall short as leaders for two main reasons. Either they were never taught how to lead, communicate and build relationships; or they were never empowered to focus on their individual strengths to lead.

Even with this default pattern of leading I saw a lot of winning and 'success', but it came at the cost of resentment, discontentment and burnout. It's led me to wonder if success without fulfillment is really worthwhile. Personally, I don't think so, but that's for you to decide. It's possible for any method to lead to winning, but if you want to strive for true greatness and fulfillment it takes a deeper level of commitment.

Education around the topic of leadership is nothing novel. It's been around for ages and yet it still seems to be one of the fastest spreading genres of personal & professional growth. Which begs the question:

what are we missing? My take on the missing puzzle piece is centered around individualization. While I believe most, who are speaking or teaching on the subjects of leadership have good intentions, many forget the most important ingredient: context. Because knowledge without context means nothing. So, we've got to redefine what it means to be a leader through this lens of understanding the individual and the team in connection together.

It's often been said "Nobody cares how much you know, until they know how much you care." But it's so much more than just knowing how much you care, it's knowing who you are, how you operate and how to inspire and empower others. Additionally, it's knowing the same about the people around you. For authentic leadership to be fully alive it requires a dynamic process. There is no set way of leading, rather it must consistently flow through the path of least resistance. Being effective isn't about getting people to fall in line, it's about uniquely empowering them to want to give their best effort; for them to be their best and want to make others better.

Ultimately growth occurs at the speed of trust. I'm going to share how to increase your speed of trust through my core framework of redefining leadership which states: before you can lead others, you need to lead yourself, and before you can lead yourself you need to know yourself.

KNOW THYSELF

As I mentioned I left college athletics in 2018 after reaching a tipping point. I was burned out, broke, alone and feeling hopeless. Over the course of eight months I had lived in five different cities, had four different jobs and lived in three different states across a span of 2,000 miles. I had believed this journey was to pursue my passion, but it was actually a misalignment within myself by following what I thought I 'should' be doing with my life. I took a desk job for the first time in an attempt to get back on my feet and get some experience in the business world. In my first week as a data analyst at a mechanical company I knew this wasn't the place for me, but it wasn't until six months later that the dam began to burst internally.

I was sick and tired of feeling sick and tired. I realized that the way I had been thinking and living not only wasn't working, but it might destroy me. The Orlando airport was across the highway from our office and I vividly remember sitting in a parking lot watching the planes fly by. I would daydream about where those people were going, longing for the freedom of a fresh start and the autonomy to do things my way. I remember thinking to myself "is this really it"?

For the first time in my life I started to believe the narrative that you couldn't do what you love and make good money. This feeling of hopelessness spread deeper through my body on a daily basis until I couldn't take it anymore. I had a paradigm shift, and this new thought popped in my head: "Well if this is rock bottom it can't get worse, right?" I leaned into that question and decided to throw a hail Mary and go after what I really wanted to do with my life. Regardless of how impossible it felt at the time.

The short version is that I invested in myself and hired coaches (with thousands of dollars I didn't have at the time) to create the business and life I didn't think was possible. And it was through that process that I began understanding the power of my first tenet of leadership: know thyself.

I hired a coach thinking he was going to help me create and grow a successful fitness business, which he did, but I had no idea how my life would change through the personal development aspect of his program. After six weeks of vision casting, mindset, reflection and breaking through limiting beliefs I became a completely different person–in the best possible way.

I soon realized that I had lived most of my life in the survival mentality: focusing on what I didn't want to happen. I was so caught up in the 'shoulds' of the world by trying to live in a way that would please others. I had never really asked myself what I wanted, or more importantly who I wanted to be in the world. Which was the biggest reason I didn't feel success.

After getting clear on who I was and what I wanted, not only did I show up with more confidence, but that energy was polarizing to the people around me. Instantly I was attracting more clients, having deeper connections and growing my business with less effort.

This was one of the few times since knowing that I wanted to pursue the field of strength & conditioning that a path felt so right for me, I knew deep down I was finally on my destined trajectory. There's something deeply satisfying in truly knowing you are in the right place and following your gut even when it doesn't make sense to the rest of the world.

This is why the path to leadership, success and empowerment really starts with creating your own identity. Because if you don't know who you are, you won't know how you fit in (with the world, your team, in relationships).

And if you don't define yourself, somebody else will.

At the beginning, I knew Exercise Science was the route for me, but the key component I was missing was trying to be like the other coaches ahead of me. It wasn't so much the "what" of my career that was missing, it was the "how" of stepping into this field, in a way that was in alignment with my identity.

That pursuit of trying to be like other people led to my mediocrity as a leader for years because I wasn't showing up with integrity to my greater purpose. All because I never took the time to define myself and explore who I wanted to be or how I wanted to show up in the world.

LEAD YOURSELF

Once you know who you are (your identity), what's important to you (your values) and how you want to live these things out (your purpose) it's about living in a way that is in alignment by holding yourself accountable.

One of the leaders I admired most, is a strength coach I worked with in college football. Now when I say admired, I'm still not even sure if I even liked the guy. He was rough around the edges, demanding and abrasive. But I've never experienced personal responsibility, honesty and ownership at such a deep level.

At the time I was at the bottom of the pecking order on staff and there were multiple occasions where myself and other coaches didn't meet the expectations of this coach. A lack of execution in certain areas often led to beratement by the head coach in front of the entire team, personnel and staff. It was demoralizing and embarrassing to say the least.

However, what always resulted was this coach (unlike many others) taking extreme ownership, by asking himself the question: What could I have done better as a leader? While holding us accountable for not meeting his expectations he would at the same time reflect how he could have better prepared or communicated. He chose to take part of the blame in the failure of these events every single time.

It was really inspiring the way he took ownership of his part, and how it led to better communication, connection and systems in place each week to create more cohesiveness as a team.

Leading yourself is ultimately having the ability to hold yourself to the same standard you would expect of others. Once you know your identity, values and purpose it's about living it out through personal accountability, responsibility and extreme ownership. If you can't be honest with yourself and own your actions, you'll never be able to lead others. It is because my mentor was able to do this, that he not only gained my respect, but he became a leader I wanted to follow through his example, even if I wasn't sure if I even liked him.

LEAD OTHERS

When it comes to leading others it's really like putting together a puzzle. You have to take into account the bigger picture and the intricacy of each different piece. If you can inspire, educate and empower the people around you, to know and lead themselves it allows the entire team to flourish synchronistically.

As I said before, growth occurs at the speed of trust. Which means it's not about creating policies or writing core values on the wall of your office to get people on board. Instead it's about connecting with people through authentic relating. When each individual can show up genuinely as themselves and compliment the strengths of others you have an unbeatable recipe for success.

When you take the time to get to know others in the same way you need to get to know yourself, it's the most powerful way to lead. You just can't lead others the same way you lead yourself because not everyone will respond to one style of leadership.

REDESIGN LEADERSHIP FOR YOU

If you have one take away from this chapter, I hope you realize the key to authentic leadership begins by defining what it means to you. I've given you a framework from my own personal journey that I believe will help guide you in this process. At the end of the day though, you are responsible for your life, happiness and the impact you have on the world.

I challenge you to break the beliefs of old ways of thinking, which no longer serve you. Redesign what leadership means for you. This is your permission slip to live uniquely and unapologetically as yourself because what's best for you and the world around you is being fully you. Get to know yourself, learn to trust your gut and lean into fear. Because on the other side of fear is a life worth living.

TAYLOR SLEAFORD

Taylor Sleaford is a Life and Leadership Coach, and host of the Fully Human Podcast who helps Entrepreneurs & High Achieving Professionals optimize their life to have freedom while getting more results. He uses personal development as the groundwork to live a great life and increase career success. His unique background in athletics has led him to a comprehensive approach of developing the whole human from the inside out.

Working in the highest levels, at Colorado State and Clemson University, with professional athletes and corporate executives, Taylor has firsthand insight into the mindset, leadership and team dynamics of elite performers. After recognizing the most successful individuals were the ones prioritizing personal growth, Taylor shifted from strength and conditioning to the self-development space to help people enhance all aspects of their life.

Taylor lives in Denver, Colorado and when not coaching you can find him snowboarding, mountain biking, trail running or chasing the next adventure.

Website: www.taylorsleaford.com/

Instagram: @taylor_sleaford

Email: taylor@taylorsleaford.com

FOLLOWING THE INTUITIVE BREADCRUMBS

I had someone tell me seven years ago that I'd be an entrepreneur and spiritual leader. I remember sitting there, broken down and depressed, and at a big low in my life. I was a school speech therapist at the time and it was winter and my seasonal depression was in full swing. I was also in my Saturn return (the astrological equivalent of becoming an adult). I was desperate. I remember hearing these words and laughing at her; little old me? A business owner? A leader? No way. I had been so comfortable in my career and my life that at the time, I couldn't fathom beginning anything new or leading a life that was different than what was so beautifully curated in front of me. As we know though, nothing grows in our comfort zone.

Fast forward to seven years later, I have followed the nudges of my soul and I've been heart led from the very beginning. Some people have intentions to create businesses and start these entrepreneurial journeys but mine pretty much fell into my lap. Sometimes I wake up and say "how did I get here?" Cue the Talking Heads song…

It was late Winter of 2019, I had become certified in Reiki and had been on a six month awakening journey back home to myself after being woken up by literal taps on my feet from spirit to start living my purpose. I had recently moved to San Francisco, California from New York City; leaving a pension, friends, family, and a whole life behind. It was a shake up in the best way. I woke up from a dream in the middle of the night and grabbed my journal and a pen and scribbled down a few pages. The next morning, I reached for my journal to write down my daily gratitude list and before me was an outline for a women's circle. Down to the details of what items I'd bring, what would happen and the feelings evoked from the women.

In hindsight, I see that it was a channeled download from my higher self. I didn't know why this was happening but what I did know was "holy shit, I have to do this." The inner critic immediately came up to say "who are you to lead this?" "No one will come." "They'll think you're crazy." But I ignored these doubts. I didn't think of the money or how many women would come or anything except "This has to be done." I was so determined that after work that day, I began scouring free spaces in my neighborhood in San Francisco. I called up a few libraries and found one that had a space open for the day I had chosen; it landed on the evening of the new moon in Aries. I realized months later that Aries season is the beginning of the astrological new year. I was truly stepping into this version of me during a new lunar year and cycle without "consciously" knowing it. A true example of being intuitively and heart led.

I remember getting off the phone and sitting in my living room and saying aloud "I am holding a New Moon Women's Circle at this library on April 4th, 2019" I took a stroll to the library a week before the event and sat in the room. I felt called to be there, feel its energy, and connect with it before the event. I was really doing it. Did I mention I had moved to San Francisco only months prior? Not really knowing many women at all, I didn't have a goal in mind or any expectations, it just had to be done. No rhyme or reason.

The days leading up to this event, I shared on social media and texted all of a handful of women that I knew in San Francisco. There was a moment where my ego came in and said "well, they'll think that's weird or some crazy moon lady stuff." I ignored the inner critic and did it anyway. It turns out some women who I wouldn't have expected to be interested at all wound up showing up that night. That was one of my first lessons in the fact that you have no idea where someone is on their journey and what their interests are; it's only up to you to share and let people come to their own conclusions and assumptions. We aren't here to decide how people will make choices. We are the lighthouses; we get to share and spread our light regardless of who we think is or isn't listening.

I remember that day so vividly. I got home from work and prepared my belongings. I had typed up a guided meditation; adorable, I know. Fast forward to present day and I channel meditations off the top of my head. Bless 2019 Michelle! I remember creating a meetup account just for this event, I didn't know how many women would show up but I trusted that even if one came, it was meant to be. I got to the library and walked into the room; there was a glass wall so we didn't have complete privacy from the rest of the library and I would say it wasn't held in the most ideal of environments. But this is where my feng shui and sacred space skills began to sprout; as I was cleaning the floors, I noticed sticky crackers and gummy bears and crumbs from a Mommy and Me class that had happened earlier that afternoon. I played soft frequency sounds, set up my diffuser for essential oils and found a fake orchid plant in the room. I grabbed the plant and placed her in the middle of the circle/sacred space with oracle cards and candles. I had transformed the messy, sticky toddler play area into a warm, inviting space for women to come together and share, meditate, and journal their thoughts. Women began trickling in, some I knew, some I didn't, and soon there were twelve women in a circle waiting eagerly for me to begin this space. We were thirteen women; thirteen new moons a year, thirteen menstrual cycles a year...thirteen–the goddess number. What?!

That night sparked a movement within me, I began holding new moon ceremonies monthly and eventually moved into a loft space that a friend so graciously opened up to me. In the middle of a bustling downtown San Francisco, women came together twice a month to share and heal and lift up the collective energies. Three years later and I've held over fifty ceremonies for women, some members have even enlisted me for their bridal and baby showers. These circles became a space for women to come together and share in a way that isn't so readily available in the everyday world. In the Summer of 2019, I had an intuitive hit to do my first virtual circle while on a solo trip in Europe; I remember sitting in my Paris airbnb and streaming live to Facebook. Not realizing that half a year later, these virtual ceremonies would become a monthly sacred occurrence for dozens of women across the world during a very unpredictable and scary time.

That scary and unpredictable time has now invited the entire world into looking at things from a different perspective over the last two years. To live in a way that is congruent with all aspects of your life. To follow your deepest desires no matter what they may look like to the outside world or even to you. Our hearts are not logical; we leave that energy up to the brain. I say if it makes no sense, then it's probably the most aligned energy for you. But who is taught to follow their heart? We hear it all of the time, all of our lives yet we live in a society where from school age, we are taught to sit down, be quiet, only talk when called upon, sit at desks for hours on end, follow the rules, be in structured programs with very little space for creativity and soul. As an educator for a decade, I have seen firsthand the decline of art and music programs as well as extracurricular activities in the public school system. Children are no longer being given the opportunity to operate with the right side of their brain, the hemisphere responsible for creative activities and emotional learning. We are not taught to follow our hearts, we're taught to follow the herd. Go to school, get a job, get married, buy a house, have babies, invest in your 401k and so on and so forth. These are all beautiful goals and by no means am I downplaying any of these miraculous milestones but when was the last time you questioned the status quo? I invite you into some self reflection.

Have you sat down and asked yourself lately (or ever):

What does my heart want?

What do I desire?

What feeds me?

What lights me up?

What brings me joy?

Who brings me calm and peace and fun?

What do I love doing without an end goal or that involves anyone else's well being except my own?

I like to believe as a society we are moving towards more heart centered living and this is why entrepreneurship is becoming so much more accessible and appealing. We are moving away from old structures of hustle and grind; doing things with little integrity and misalignment with who you truly are and what your values are.

Most of us have walked around for decades not knowing who we are, what we desire, and how to live from our heart spaces because we are undoing so much of what society deems as successful and 'right.' Society right now is very much driven by ego and working from the solar plexus chakra of "I": desire and greed rather than unconditional love and collective energy for all.

The irony is that when we do things that light us up and bring us joy and we move towards this energy of vulnerability and heart, we naturally create a ripple effect into each and every person we know personally as well as everyone we interact with in our lives. It's science! Our heart spaces have a six foot electrical field around them. When we step into heart energy, we are reflections and mirrors. When you love and accept yourself, you give others permission to do the same. At times, I forget I have a business and that I'm a leader because I'm just doing what lights me up, I'm being unapologetically me. And that, in and of itself, becomes a magnet for those who also desire more for themselves. Lead with authenticity, liberate yourself from the constructs placed on you, and see the magic of your essence come alive again. I see it in my clients all the time; they are just giving themselves permission to be themselves and take off the masks that they've been wearing for decades. It's a deep homecoming.

When I embarked on a solo nomadic journey in the Winter of 2021, I had all of these expectations and ideas of what it would look like. I'd be touring the country and doing pop up events everywhere, meeting amazing people and seeing beautiful mother nature. And yes I have done a lot of those things but I also was healing. I was called into a deeper layer of shedding and releasing all attachments of my former identity, including what my business started out from. I was no longer the Michelle who facilitated women's circles in libraries, I was now a woman with a podcast, sharing her truth unapologetically and inspiring her female clients who were moving through transitional phases of their lives and releasing the old programming and labels.

Every chapter of your life will invite you into deeper shedding and revealing of who you really are and who you came here to be on this Earth at this critical time of existence. It can be confronting, scary, vulnerable as hell, and also exciting. We get to hold multiple emotions at one time; you can be excited and also really scared! You can be grieving and also feeling waves of happiness. You also get to reinvent yourself each and every day of your life. You have to be willing to leave everything behind to follow your heart and your truest north. When it makes no sense and you're attempting to rationalize it? Yeah, those are the ideas and experiences worth listening to. Your only competition is you and the you of yesterday. Look how far you've come in the last month, six months, two years? We have all shifted exponentially since March 2020 and you get to reflect on that and keep going!

Take a moment from reading this and write down your accomplishments over the last two years and what you're proud of. They don't have to be Earth shattering things; something as small as observing your thoughts can be an accomplishment! Everything begins with awareness. Liberating ourselves can feel uncomfortable like a snake shedding its skin or a caterpillar becoming complete mush in its cocoon. We have no idea what it's going to look like or what we will be at the end of the transformation but we trust and we surrender and we let go of expectations and we lead with our hearts. When everyone else is telling you to follow that path, you forge your own. You ebb and flow with the currents of your personal journey. It's your mistakes you get to live, it's your experiences you get to have, and ultimately, it's your life you get to lead. We are all leaders and main characters in our own lives; just by being unabashedly you, you grant openness and vulnerability and non judgment to every soul around you. It's not up to you whether people are inspired by you or triggered by your transformation; remember, if you're understood and liked by every person, you're not living in alignment with your soul.

To me, being a leader doesn't mean that I'm above anyone else. I remind everyone I work with to kick the pedestal out from under me if there is one because we are all in this together. A leader leads with vulnerability, with bravery, with not being afraid to fail, and releasing others' judgments of what it may look like. A leader goes first. A leader releases their own judgments of what it may look like. We get to step out of the idea that failure is wrong or bad; when you are creating a new path, it gets to be messy and unapologetic. Quitting is frowned upon in our society and quite frankly it's one of the greatest gifts. It's all in the journey and how it unfolds, not necessarily the destination. The entire journey is the destination. We get to be with each and every step of the process. We get to allow the twists and turns to make the story because you never know what chapters of your life are unfolding so magically until it's in hindsight and maybe they were the greatest moments of your life.

HEART-CENTERED LEADERSHIP

I encourage everyone to get quiet, take a few deep breaths, place a hand over your heart, come back to this sacred space, and listen to what your inner knowing has to say. Getting out of our head and dropping into our heart and its innate wisdom. It's crucial in this game called life and your heart will never lead you astray from your path and the callings of your soul. Let it make no sense and trust the unbecoming of your life. Lead with your heart, lead your life.

MICHELLE BADAGLIACCA

Michelle Badagliacca is a spiritual leader and awakening coach for women. Michelle helps intuitive women and female entrepreneurs transform their lives and create heart centered businesses through energetic alignment and intuitive, spiritual practices. Michelle has held 50+ women's circles and workshops, is a certified breath-work coach, and a Reiki Master and Teacher. Michelle was inspired to do this work because through her personal journey back home to herself, she knows how important it is for women to embody and reclaim their power, pleasure, and prosperity through their innate feminine energy to change the world. Michelle is solo traveling across the USA as a digital nomad.

Instagram: @michelle.the.mystic

Website: www.michelle-badagliacca.mykajabi.com

BECOMING AT ONE

"What do you want?" asked Maleya, my hypnotherapist.

Silence. I searched within. Still, I heard nothing.

"I don't know," I answered, discouraged.

"No one's ever asked you that before. Including you," Maleya gently explained.

THE HEART

I've been working with Maleya, a gifted hypnotherapist, for several months now. Through hypnosis, she's guided me to places in my psyche I've never been. Places that were so real and raw that I'd return to my waking state feeling cracked open. I'd been longing for this level of honesty. In hypnosis, I saw myself, **really** saw myself.

I'd worn my mask for so long that I became it—the high achiever who always did great. Hustle, pressure, and force drove my exerted body and busy mind. Fear of failure supplied an infinite stream of adrenaline. I didn't feel lost but I was lost, living in my head, guided by a logical path to 'success' with society's arbitrary list of accomplishments.

Weaknesses were present underneath, but I was good at pretending. My ego was fragile. My temper was short. I struggled with an eating disorder. It became increasingly difficult to convince myself this perfect, shiny image was real. Yet, I did not know how to be anyone else. So, I continued overworking, overcommitting, people-pleasing, so I could prove to others (well, to myself) that I was worthy.

The mask finally broke. It was a quarrel with a friend, piled upon a lifetime of sensitivity to 'what others think', that finally did it. Throughout my entire life, I had no boundaries, not even a vague concept of what boundaries even meant. Others' thoughts about me became my own thoughts of myself. What others needed for themselves became what I needed to make happen.

Enough was enough.

I had to look underneath the cracked mask and discover myself. I wanted to see her, the true her—the messy, neat, dark, light, all of her. I didn't know how to help her because I didn't know her.

Enter hypnotherapy. Right there in Maleya's office, in her comfortable recliner, she brought me under hypnosis, and we began.

Hypnosis is a state of consciousness, where a portal between the conscious and the subconscious mind opens and there is communication, a sharing of wisdom, between the two. The conscious mind is logical while the subconscious mind is not. The gifts of logic are well-accepted. The gifts of intuition, inner wisdom, inexplicable passion, and unbridled love exist in the subconscious, with all the beautiful matters of the heart.

It is wise to honor both. In Western society, logic is reinforced and tangible results are valued. We see before we believe. The intangible, however, carries the burden of proof. Unfortunately, then, the intangible becomes easily dismissed. I internalized this emphasis on logic, leading with my head, not my heart, for a long time. It felt safe. It didn't feel real.

It was time to bring the head and heart into balance. I was so disconnected with my heart that I had no answer to the seemingly simple question "what do you want?" The answer was in there, somewhere, just locked away in a protective chamber.

Self-acceptance unlocked my heart's voice, but, oh, was it a process to get there. To encourage my heart to speak, she had to feel heard. I needed safety within myself, **from** myself, the self-judging, dismissing, and shaming. Developing a trusting relationship with my heart, anchored in compassion and kindness, was the real work.

Self-acceptance was where my story of heart-centered leadership began.

WHERE I'M FROM

My parents were Chinese-Cambodian refugees, fleeing from the Khmer Rouge regime in the 1970s. I've only heard a few of their genocide stories—the rest they prefer to bury in the past. My mom, her five sisters, and my dad survived. My grandparents and my dad's family did not.

Barely adults, my aunties and parents arrived in America. A deep breath of relief. The landmines and executions were now far behind. Then, a new reality set in. No English. No money. No parents. Another deep breath. Survival was not yet theirs. Keep running.

They took any job, did assembly line work, their bodies and spirits exhausted but survival took precedence. Money came and left–food, rent, and basic clothes. Yet, they found their reason to keep moving forward, and it was within one another. They were family, best friends, quite literally ride-or-dies. They survived because they had each other.

Fast forward eight years. I was born in Los Angeles, from their love, pain, grief, and hope. I was welcomed into this beautiful family that moved and breathed like one unit. In American individualistic culture, dependency is given a bad rap, but I saw its beauty in the threads of my family. The epitome of collectivism, my parents and aunties all cared for me like a daughter, my sister and cousins like siblings. We shared everything. Together, my parents and aunties rebuilt what the Khmer Rouge destroyed, their determination fueled by love. Their children will have what they could not.

I had a happy childhood filled with loving people, but unprocessed trauma always lurked. Anxious energy, irrational fears, and worst case scenarios. I absorbed them like a sponge. My parents were hyper-vigilant about my safety, and so I was about theirs. When I got dropped off at school, I'd feel a gripping fear that my parents would die when they left my sight—the shadows of generational wartime trauma. The world is dangerous and unpredictable. Work hard, keep your head down, stay out of trouble. We clung onto society's rulebook for success as if our lives depended on it. In a way, my parents were still running from the Khmer Rouge. I was running from their ghosts too.

THE PAVED PATH

Fight or flight was my baseline, which I channeled into every achievement. I was stellar at conforming and addicted to vanity metrics, willing all my aspirations into existence—top 10 in my high school class, my goal weight on the scale, admission to a prestigious college.

I took pride in my discipline and self-control, even if the self-control was self-destructive. Sleep-deprived, malnourished, and stressed, I wore them all like a badge of honor. I went to college at University of California, Berkeley and, of course, was pre-med. I saw many high-achieving peers push themselves this same way, but express similar sentiments of inadequacy.

Perhaps I could help other people by helping myself. To understand the inner workings of my mind, I worked in a social psychology lab. I wrote my honors' thesis on perfectionism, disordered eating, and the effectiveness of self-compassion interventions. Our ability to shape our minds piqued my interest, but no one I knew made a living out of that. So, it was relegated to casual dinner conversations. My heart had given me a nudge. Like always, I brushed right past.

I strayed from pre-med but still searched for a paved road. I found occupational therapy (OT), earned a clinical doctorate, and practiced for seven years. The therapeutic use of occupations (our meaningful, everyday activities) sounded like a wonderful confluence of physical and mental health—just my jam. I worked in neurorehabilitation, specifically stroke and brain injuries, and studied the brain in the context of physical disabilities. My colleagues became family, I was committed to my patients, and I did good work.

I'd made it. Security and stability were in the bag, along with work I found fulfilling. The years passed. I loved each one. With each year, though, it became increasingly clear.

I had become a square peg that no longer fit into this round hole.

It was time to stop making myself fit.

THE DEPARTURE

"I'm standing in a forest, paths radiating out from this circle I'm standing in, paths going in all directions. I can't clearly see down the paths. I'm uneasy."

My client, Rose, was under hypnosis, describing where her mind took her. She's been feeling stuck, stagnant with her life.

I guided her to consult her wise being, in her case, a Cheshire cat.

"He's hopping around some tree branches above me. He sees I'm distressed. He says 'there are many right ways, trust yourself, any one is better than staying here.'"

I brought her out of hypnosis. She had found her own answer.

Next session came. I took her under hypnosis. Immediately, she found herself enjoying the forest view, the Cheshire cat basking in the sun. I asked where she was. "I'm down one of those paths. I don't even know which one. It doesn't matter. I'm happy here."

She started making moves. She relocated to New York, loved this change, and is one step closer to her dream career.

We don't always need to know how our path will look. With trust in your heart, just go.

* * *

"So, HMI, huh?" Maleya said, sitting across her desk.

My hypnotherapy with Maleya had profound, lasting impacts. Astonished, I wanted to know more. At first, it was an intellectual curiosity. I'd gone to several free workshops at Hypnosis Motivation Institute (HMI), Maleya's alma mater, and was on the edge of my seat each class. I felt magnetized to this place. I enrolled and my rigorous training began. I worked full-time in OT while moonlighting with hypnotherapy. My years as an OT helped it all make more sense.

Science and art were in harmony at HMI. I learned the evolutionary and neurological background of our conscious and subconscious minds, principles of counseling and interviewing, and therapeutic planning. I took on clients as an intern. I learned to artfully influence conscious states, and to use metaphors and symbols to guide clients through their psyche. Anything seemed possible.

Inevitably, fear came. Reality check. Hypnotherapy is not a traditional path. There is no space carved out in traditional settings. So, most hypnotherapists are entrepreneurs, carving their own space. Traditional is safe, traditional is pre-approved. Hypnotherapy is neither.

Then came shame. Hypnosis was unheard of for most people I knew, except for stage show entertainment. Hell, even I was skeptical before hypnotherapy changed my life. My world was healthcare, my friends from Silicon Valley tech, my family never went to therapy. To my tribe, hypnotherapy was woo-woo. Kumbaya. Unsubstantiated pseudoscience. The expanded feeling of grand possibilities contracted. With hypnotherapy, I came alive in an unprecedented way, yet I was ashamed of this huge part of myself.

'I'm just dabbling,' I told myself. I'm not leaving OT.

I did not just dabble. I immersed myself in this world, visiting campus five days per week, practicing on peers, and doing extra weekend certifications. After a year, I graduated with honors and was recognized for my clinical and academic achievements. I still received hypnotherapy one-to-one to find my courage, acknowledge the voices of fear and shame, and amplify the voice of my heart. My belief in hypnotherapy grew, as did my belief in myself.

It was magical to see it all come together—the healing power of language, changing conscious states, and transformation. Well, *trance*-formation. It was artful, it was technical, it was emotional, it was beautiful. I was in awe. I loved it, I was good at it, and I felt deep, permanent shifts. My clients did too. We designed our own minds and, subsequently, designed our own lives. My heart's call grew louder. "Time to leap," my heart whispered.

I walked away from a six-figure salary, pension, and an established field in healthcare. I walked straight towards a stigmatized profession. I launched my hypnotherapy business, with no entrepreneurial experience. My phone lit up. A prior OT mentor with a judgmental text. My dad tells me, fear in his voice, "You're making a mistake, go back to government work." I have and will continue to face raised eyebrows, rushed judgements, and skeptical questions about mind control and the swinging pocket watch. Deep breath in on the mantra "my mission is louder than my fear." I joined the cause, advancing credibility for this powerful, subconscious work. I left 'traditional' behind.

ATONEMENT

I have a complex relationship with my frenemy (friend + enemy) named Control. Because of Control, I was on top of every game but only played games I could safely win. Entrepreneurship is the wild, wild west. When I am my own leader, there are no pre-established guidelines, and Control did not like that.

My dad, a genuinely compassionate soul, is plagued with PTSD, easily startled, irritated, and angered. Control was this refugee's refuge - keep everything predictable, new places and new people bring trouble. My mother, a natural and gifted caregiver, loves people and travel, but is perpetually worried, over-involved in our choices, and constantly exhausted. Control was also her refuge—make sure to take care of everyone else so they don't struggle. Here I come, their daughter, a melding of them both, the paradoxical stressed adventurer with a savior complex.

My parents are my heroes, surviving more than I can imagine, hearts staying kind throughout the atrocities witnessed. They've done their best with the awareness they have, but freedom from generational trauma lies with me. Freedom is not free.

Cycle-breaking work is painful. The heart-forward choice of writing this chapter and you, my dear readers, inspired me to dive down into unchartered depths of healing. I journaled continuously for this project and the following thoughts came, along with a flood of pain.

Although bonded by a deep well of love, I talk to my parents across a wide chasm of cultural, generational, and language differences. Their fear, our fear, had many faces. I resented them all. I fought against them, fought against myself, and realized I was fighting the same damn thing the whole time. After all, the attributes that I resisted in them, I saw in me. Self-acceptance and self-love would not be complete without accepting my parents.

It was painful to break down my walls, stacked high with ego and pride. After all, I was breaking down a part of myself. Deep down, I knew, if I could have a second chance at any one thing in this lifetime, it'd be to grow up with a better relationship with them. Rigid expectations, of them and of me, came down with that wall, and the tight grip of Control released a little more. It was a rugged process.

Emotional pain is physical for me. The breakdown of Control, the glue that held me together my whole life, physically hurt my body, an aching pain in my chest that lasted for days. All that previously restricted energy of unprocessed generational trauma found a newly open path. All the pain I blocked away, in them, in me, now rushed through my body.

The pain and tears did subside as they always do, and that rapid flow of energy slowed. Then, a glimpse; freedom and connection flowed in after pain. Through the lens of a compassionate eye, I could see our imperfections, suffering, love, and humanness flow through too. I let it all in. If pain is the up-front cost for this vulnerable, true, and intimate connection to my parents, to myself, to my heart…I'll pay.

The rebuilding began, the wall now rubble, and stone by stone, a bridge slowly began to form.

* * *

WHEN I CREATE A SAFE, loving home within myself, the vast unknown becomes a place of possibility. Leading with the heart also means leading with love, with self-love at the helm. When I'm kind to myself, I am rejection proof. Bigger leaps. Pure curiosity. More exploration. I come alive.

With self-love in my core, unconditional love streams towards my clients. My clients feel safe with me because I feel safe with me. I trust myself to guide them so they trust me to guide them too. I hold an unwavering belief for our process, for them. They borrow this belief until it becomes their own.

Heal others by first healing yourself. I learned to align my own chaotic energies—my mentors showed me how. I directed my fire, initially wild and untamed, into a warm, illuminating, productive force. I removed shame from my shadows and came to accept all of me, transforming my fragmented self into a unified one. When I gave myself permission to be myself, clients gave themselves permission to do the same.

Self-leadership came first. Then, I effectively led others. Penelope, who funneled her rage into building healthy boundaries. In hypnotherapy, her anger transformed into a beam of light, shooting forward from her hand. Charles, who, under hypnosis, redirected his parental resentment towards comforting his six-year-old self. He is now bravely writing a letter to his parents, showing his vulnerability in an unprecedented way. I watched them learn to take control of their own unwieldy energy and turn it into focused, effective power. They began building a safe home for themselves, within themselves. Just like me, they started hearing their hearts. They started taking risks. They started coming alive.

The home called 'Myself' was my journey's destination this whole time, and Oneness was always the goal. There is a symbiosis in all parts of me that I was destined to create. Previously antagonistic, but now coming into harmony. Control-Surrender. Security-Freedom. Chinese-American. OT-Hypnotherapy. Pain-Love. Self-Daughter. Logic-Intuition. Shadow-Light.

The word Atonement, broken down, is At-ONE-ment. Becoming At One with ourselves is the journey of our lives. Be heart-forward as you walk your path, leading yourself with love. It's a movement and you're part of it. My mentors led with their hearts and then I could. I led with my heart and then my clients could. You being your unique self gives others permission to be uniquely them. I'm sending my love to you, ALL parts of you, while you walk each step of your path—the bumpy, the smooth, the winding, the straight. I acknowledge your courage with each step, even if the destination isn't always clear. I'm walking my path too, in a way, walking right there with you, on this journey we're all in together to become At One.

CLARISSA TU

Clarissa Tu is a certified hypnotherapist, helping those struggling with anxiety change default patterns, tap into their inner resources, and take empowered action through hypnotic tools. Throughout her life, Clarissa has been interested in neuroscience, which has translated into her passion for hypnotherapy. She also has a clinical Doctorate in Occupational Therapy and practiced as an occupational therapist in neurorehabilitation prior to finding hypnotherapy. She became fascinated with it after witnessing the powerful and permanent effects it had on her own life as a client. She has since transitioned fully into entrepreneurship with her business, HypnoClarity, using a holistic approach to heal the mind, body, and spirit with hypnosis. Driven by her own healing journey, Clarissa's mission is to guide others in elevating consciousness and create a life of their design.

Website: www.hypnoclaritytherapy.com

Instagram: @clarissa_tu

Facebook: www.facebook.com/hypnoclaritytherapy

*LinkedI*n: www.linkedin.com/in/clarissa-tu

YOUR IMPACT IS IN YOUR CHARACTER

WOUNDS TO WISDOM

I am a highly sensitive, intuitive and creative empath who experiences the world with a fine attunement. I move most naturally through the subtle and refined lens of beauty, richness, and the clear simplicity of the senses. Deeply carried by music, architecture, the arts, culture, and our natural world, I've learned to accentuate these attributes as well as protect them.

I learned to protect them because they weren't always seen or nurtured. I was raised by an emotionally unavailable father who deeply loved me yet was limited in his ability to show it in a healthy way. I was raised by a loving, kind, unconditionally supportive, and empathetic mother who often put her needs aside and silenced her voice in order to keep the peace. Raised in a military family, I moved every three years, which interrupted the nurturance of a stable physical base in which to develop, explore, and expand from. Each time I started to get settled in myself, with friends, and my environment, it was time to move again. This combined psychological, emotional and physical unpredictability resulted in trauma and a dysregulated nervous system that impacted me for many years. My father wound presented as a high tolerance for hurtful behavior, exhaustive attempts to repair other's harmful actions, and overcompensation for another's unchanged behavior. I often thought that if I did enough, it would change. I learned this wasn't the case.

With a degree in Psychology and twenty-three years of age, I experienced a gradual but undeniable turning point. I embarked on a journey that led to a transformational path of self-discovery, wisdom, and ultimately, wholeness and freedom. While I was still my spirited, strong-willed self, I was struggling with anxiety, low self-belief, and low-worth behavior amidst my parent's divorce, graduating college, health diagnoses, and underneath it all, deep seated grief that was trying to make itself known.

This return to wholeness included study, training and healing through various modalities, wisdom traditions, career and leadership experiences, and the continual cultivation of my own self-trust, intuition, and a return to who I was without the interference of my trauma.

If we want to rise above our fear and conditioned tendency to play small, feel fully alive, and create extraordinary lives, we must do the inner work, move beyond conditional confidence and surface level spirituality, and integrate it into our daily beliefs, actions, and ways of being in the world.

This is how legendary leaders are created—through brave, consistent, and open hearted acts.

MY DESIRE FOR YOU

We all want to feel that our lives have meaning, purpose, and value. We all want to feel that our time here is worthwhile.

For those expressing your gifts, *keep going.*

For those of you on your way, *keep going.*

For those of you lost and confused, *keep going.*

Don't let your gifts die inside of you. I don't want that for you, and I surely don't want that for our planet and your loved ones. We need you. We need your voice. We need your story. It's the bridge humanity needs for collective empowerment and true interdependence. There are people waiting to be in your corner as you take brave and vulnerable steps to become more of who you really are. You are not alone.

From across the resounding miles, I am one of them...

YOUR IMPACT IS IN YOUR CHARACTER

It's often portrayed that having an impact on the world is achieved through sweeping visions, global innovation, and ambitious undertakings that set one apart from the average person–through the attending of top tier masterminds or globe trotting to exclusive symposiums. This is certainly one way to enact leadership and these types of leaders are needed to affect change at a certain level. And, heart-led leadership is an opportunity to live in accordance with your truest values everyday, and thus impact change firstly in your own life and therefore, in the lives of those around you.

Whether you are a parent devoting all you have to raising a healthy family, a globally recognized thought leader delivering groundbreaking speeches to thousands of fellow change agents, or working at the local cafe offering kindness to each customer that orders a cup of coffee, your *true impact is in your character.*

Your true impact is in how you live, how you love, how you parent, how you treat others, how you engage with the world and integrally, how you engage with yourself. We are often shown an outdated, distorted model of leadership, one displaying power over others, serving through martyrdom, and appealing to others through manipulative charm and a well groomed ego. Through heart-led leadership, we learn it's about *brave, vulnerable and sustainable service,* giving while also receiving, and serving through modeling exemplary care and appreciation of self and others while living in accordance with one's values. In this way, we redefine leadership to be a vibrant blooming gesture that touches all we do, rather than a need to feel powerful, in illusory control, and worthy of approval.

We let go of the story of who we are, and become who we *really* are, committed to evolving over the course of our lives.

Working on our inner game, cultivating healthy power and emotional, intellectual, and spiritual agency is what will inevitably provide the scaffolding in which true leadership is sustained. The ill-informed hunger for self-importance through acquiring ever surmounting certifications, accolades, promotions, and the like has become a disease that renders the individual even more susceptible to a fragile self if any of those external gains are stripped away. It is not a foundation on which true self-leadership and mentorship can be based, since it often hinges on external validation and standardized success to affirm internal worth, which inevitably undermines our capacity to build true self-belief and self-trust if that outside of us, which it often does, changes.

Heart-led leadership is the opportunity to forego the societally encouraged notion that we prove our worth through what we achieve. Instead, it's an invitation to reclaim our fundamental value by uncovering and living into our true nature, restoring the connection to our body's wisdom, developing intimacy with our inner selves, and modeling that we can be mission driven individuals doing brave things in the world while taking impeccable care of ourselves and in turn, those we love and serve.

It is a way of being, informed by generative, inspired action, integrity, conviction in one's value, and the equal value of others. It is never about asserting power over, yet inspiring empowerment between all parties—an assets-based approach that organizes social engagement around strengths, gifts, and a field of possibility.

BUILDING A LEGACY

Let's take a look at building a legacy. Legacy is often seen as something that is retrospective, something that an individual leaves behind, and it is. I offer the idea that it is also an active conversation, a living song of our lives that is informed by our thoughts, our choices, and our actions, now. It is a thread that undulates through time, impacted by the deeds of our lineage, and is ever informing the generations to come.

If we follow the silent script that only financially wealthy, stereotypically successful people can foster a true legacy, we disenfranchise ourselves, ultimately contributing to a falsely conditioned and self perpetuating world view that money equals power, power equals success, and hence, we are helpless to create change, let alone positive change without them.

When we renegotiate our personal relationship to legacy and our agency to create one aside from material assets, we call back our power and accept responsibility towards creating a world we want to love and live in, starting with our inner world.

Stephen Jenkinson, author and former Director of Palliative Care at Mount Sinai Hospital in Toronto, Canada, the Harvard trained cultural activist speaks to an idea in the documentary film *Griefwalker* that through his experience with over 1,000 patients on their deathbeds, most people aren't primarily afraid of dying per say; they're afraid of no one carrying their legacy forth. I beg that this legacy is beyond transactional assets, and is housed in the assets of the heart—our values, traditions, and qualities—the imprint that makes us uniquely ourselves.

We are the ancestors of the future.

BECOME THE IMPECCABLE LEADER OF YOUR OWN LIFE

The person who wants to become the unabashed leader of their own life must first embrace becoming one thing. It is what all heart-led leaders have in common: *Connection*. They are committed to the continual process of connecting to themselves, their worth, their value, their voice, their strength, their bodies, and areas of growth. They are aware that leadership does not happen in a silo and urges us to be in thoughtful collaboration with others in order to truly affect change. The heart-led leader knows that without a good team, emotional intelligence, and the capacity to reflect and take responsibility for their shortcomings, their ability to sustainably lead and learn is limited.

Becoming the leader of your own life does not require you to assume traditional leadership through a career. Rather, it is an invitation to move through the world in touch with your body's wisdom, cultivating self-knowing, and an open-hearted personal power that expresses and offers your gifts to the world. We're here to experience a rich quality of life that does more than look good, it also *feels good*. And, not only does it feel good, but it feels right—*right for us*.

Whereas behaviors found through outdated leadership models breed separation and espouse fear based attempts to gain control, connection is the salve that heals us, empowers others, and inspires collective greatness and wonder. It helps move us beyond the epidemic of internalized oppression, shame, judgment, comparison, and isolation.

GRACE, RESILIENCE & INNER STRENGTH

In order to amplify your voice and create lasting impact, cultivating these three components are exceedingly encouraged: Grace, Resilience and Inner Strength. This is quite the opposite of what is often found in toxic work environments where bullying, persuasive charm, manipulation, unappreciation, and negligence becomes the acceptable norm.

Definition of *Grace*: Elegance or beauty of form, manner, motion, or action; simple elegance or refinement of movement; courteous goodwill.

Grace is the commitment to move with care and elegance, with a refinement to one's actions and speech. It extends a good nature to others, presuming positive intent unless communicated or displayed otherwise. Sustainable relations require grace time and time again. When we're held to unrealistic, transactional records of perceived mistakes and errors, it creates a lose-lose situation, perpetuating a disempowering model that elicits an oscillation between a victim, villain, and a hero.

Definition of *Resilience*: The capacity to recover quickly from difficulties, the process of successfully adapting to challenging life experiences, through mental, emotional, and behavioral flexibility and adjustment to external and internal demands.

Resilience is our ability to withstand stressors and adapt in such a way that doesn't over personalize our experiences or limit our capacity to recover. Resilience is the inner elasticity that allows us to lead ourselves through hard things and show up to life's challenges without collapsing. We will fall apart from time to time, yet when we continually struggle to face life's experiences with strength, we diminish our capacity to grow. Resilience also applies to interpersonal relationships and our ability to bounce back from inevitable hardships, to grant grace to others, informing the longevity and sustainability of our connections.

Definition of *Inner Strength*: Integrity of character; resoluteness of will; core strength of a person.

Inner strength is the backbone that allows us to navigate a challenging world with challenging experiences and people. It is a way of being that allows us to lean on ourselves with a resourcefulness that aids courage in taking risks and inspires the capacity to live bravely.

Inner strength is the part of us, when combined with grace and compassion, that knows how to put things in perspective, and fosters a stable environment in which others feel safe enough to blossom in our presence. Inner strength is not to be mistaken for pushing through, which we sometimes need to do yet ideally not as a default mechanism for abandoning our needs. Inner strength welcomes the healing of past trauma and release of old wounds that disrupts the natural, self-stabilizing intelligence of a regulated nervous system and buoyant, steady self.

REDEFINING OUR RELATIONSHIP WITH PRODUCTIVITY

Productivity in the western world is often synonymous with undermining our needs, overriding our intuition, and getting the job done at all costs. This relentless work ethic has provided us with countless opportunities, innovative advances, and inspiring standards of excellence. And, there is a dark side to this hyper-independent status quo. Unconscious and unmet needs can often be revealed in our seeking of approval, poor boundaries, wearing of false identities in order to belong, fear of speaking up or asking for help, and self sacrifice as a commitment to the cause.

As we transition into a more sustainable way in the world, we begin to master the craft of being human: honoring our cycles and rhythms, welcoming all parts of ourselves to sit at the table, exercising self-worth and self-trust, cultivating healthy boundaries, and communicating our needs.

When we honor what we need, we are in essence being productive because it allows us to continue showing up with energy, inner resources, and self-respect.

IN THE REAL WORLD

As the saying goes, it's often the hardest lessons that teach us the most. In my case, fast forward well into my adulthood, I unknowingly entered a job with a toxic boss. I initially liked this person, gave them the benefit of the doubt, and allowed her strategic charm to do what it was intended to do, be a tool for seduction. Increasingly unable to withhold harsh judgements and criticisms, she would flippantly show a hospitable side to the world and an impatient and ill-mannered side to us. From the beginning, her leadership was devoid of appreciation for our hard work. At first it didn't bother me. I knew the value of my work well enough that I thought I didn't need to be complimented or affirmed for my work. But that's not true.

No one is exempt from the nutrient of appreciation.

Over time, her callous nature became more abrasive, as my colleagues and I walked on eggshells around her, slowly drained more and more each day. I finally quit, and over a relatively short period of time before and after, my colleagues had also quit.

I got out. It wasn't without repercussions–I was deeply depleted, burnt out, my health was suffering, and self esteem bruised.

Unfortunately, this is what happens when quality people who do good work are not valued, and moreover, those in leadership positions don't have the skills to sustainably and empathetically lead.

With compassionate truth, many leaders and managers do not get the support they need. They aren't trained how to lead, and frankly, many are not emotionally suited for the job.

This is the result of toxic, bullying leadership. Sadly, it runs rampant and is partially the consequence of unhealed, wounded inner children now stored in adult bodies. We are not meant to work, live or love in environments that leave us feeling small and less than, questioning our value and contributions, and chasing insatiable demands. It is hard to function in a work culture where goals are obscure, values are irrelevant, roles and boundaries are ambiguous, and communication is passive aggressive.

From a neuroscience standpoint, that's not how quality work is created. Quality work is created when our prefrontal cortex is online, allowing for executive functioning, creative thinking, attuned communication, empathy, fear modulation, intuition, and emotional regulation. A non-threatening environment is a required baseline in order to sustainably operate from this part of the brain. In short, toxic leadership can activate the amygdala, the part of the limbic system that regulates emotion and processes threatening and fearful stimuli, in turn shutting down our prefrontal cortex and activating fight, flight, freeze or fawn stress responses. As you might imagine, the more this behavior occurs, the less tolerable we are to life's stressors.

It's common to feel helpless, like there is no other choice, or perhaps one is in an unconscious trauma response, where the current stimuli is reminiscent of an earlier adverse experience. This is why support is needed. Burnout is real, and there is another way *(cue Heart-Centered Leadership!)*

I get it. Life is expensive. We have bills to pay. There are always reasons not to change; *'the economy is bad', 'times are tough'.* Yes, and that is precisely when we need more good leaders! Sometimes, we must go first. Whether stuck and frustrated, in burnout recovery, in transition, or thriving and ready for more, we can rarely do this alone. As a cornerstone of my work, I've developed a comprehensive *(and brave, can't get around bravery as we move towards our dreams!)* approach in the spirit of important transitions, in career, life, and self.

THE INTEGRATED SELF

The following framework is a portion of my approach developed to lead clients through a myriad of transitions and into skillful heart-led leadership. Although it can be a linear process, it's often not and requires agility as we traverse these concepts in real time.

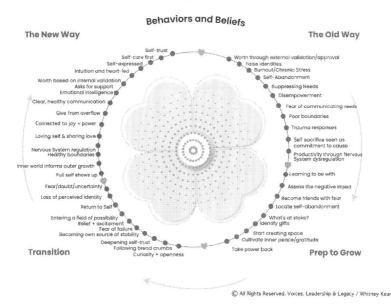

I have walked myself (sometimes on my knees) through countless transitions, opportunities to grow and what I have found is this: the more we lean into *all* of who we are–our fears, anxieties, and doubts, the more access we have to our joy, purpose, expression, wisdom and ultimately–freedom. We can do hard things and do them well. We are here to expand into our brilliance with joy and aliveness. We are here to have courageous conversations and feel closer to those we love as a result. We are here to find safety in our bodies, strength in our vulnerability, joy in our expression, and richness in our lives.

WHITNEY KEAR

Whitney Kear is an Executive Coach and Mentor, Intuitive, Podcast Host, Speaker, and founder of Voices, Leadership & Legacy. With a background in Psychology and 15+ years combined in Non-Profit Communications, Media, Development, Event Production and Self Development, her impeccable wisdom, warmth, depth and breadth serves as a powerful catalyst in the reclamation of the voice and the expression of the full self, offering compassionate and clear counsel back to one's innate wisdom and power. Her work includes roles with Case Western's Fowler Center for Business as an Agent of World Benefit, The Mingei Legacy Resource Foundation, and Californians for the Arts, among others.

Working with mission-driven leaders, creatives, and companies to realize big, bold, and brave things in the world while taking impeccable care of themselves, Whitney presents a model to bridge emotionally intelligent heart-led leadership with a rich, vibrant and fulfilled quality of life, informed by 15 years of study, training and self development.

Based in Colorado, Whitney is a singer, recording artist, dancer, animal lover, and lover of all things Italy.

Website: www.whitneykear.com

Website: www.voicesleadershiplegacy.com

Facebook Group: The Heart Led Leadership Collective

Podcast: Voices, Leadership & Legacy

The Integrated Self Approach: www.whitneykear.com/the-integrated-self

THE NEW AMERICAN DREAM: SHARING THE HEART OF THE MATTER

"I'm never sure if you're calling to announce you're the CEO of a company or running off to join the circus," my mom would say. She was always half joking, half nervous every time I called with some new, grandiose life plan. To be fair both paths were, and still are, equally likely.

One week, I would tell her about my plans of becoming a top-level sales executive overseeing large teams at high-profiting companies. Next, I'd share dreams of becoming a floral farmer off-grid where I could read spiritual books and do inner work. "That sounds like a lot," she'd say to both options and move on to the next subject like her latest furniture remodeling project.

At one point, these conversations sounded different. In her generation, safety and stability were the golden values of achievement. They were signs that you had 'made it' in the proverbial American Dream. As the daughter of a blue-collar worker, she had a hard time understanding my post-college graduation plans. I was turning down a secure job with a prestigious lobbying firm. Instead, I would join forces with six men in an apartment-sized office building to help grow a software start-up—something I was neither experienced nor qualified to do. She struggled to see why I would move 1,500 miles across the country to a city I had never visited and was baffled years later when I told her I was quitting my six-figure salaried job to take a 10-month sabbatical traveling in nature. Though somewhere between the years, she either got used to my wandering mind and eccentric heart or was exhausted from trying to keep up.

In the early years of my sales career, I was a sponge. I mimicked what I heard on calls from brilliant conversationalists I called mentors and echoed their forthcoming negotiation tactics. The paychecks proved their style worked, but it took me nearly three years of chasing adrenaline highs and burnout cycles to realize I needed to find my way. I craved my own style of selling, my own way of BEing in business.

From that point forward, I started weaving together my product knowledge and energetic intuition. I lead calls in a kind of confidence unique to only me. I opened meetings with intentions instead of agendas, met executives from Salesforce and Verizon in neon pink blazers and purple hair, and led internal meetings on creating conscious cultures. Besides building incredible rapport with prospects and customers, I quickly became the top-performing sales rep at our company making consistent six-figure salaries. Looking back, it's hard to say if I was too young and naive to realize how many rules of traditional business I was breaking, or too bold to care.

The reality though, was my success had little to do with daring outfits and quirky language. Instead, I was learning to finally integrate my worlds of business leadership and heart-centric living. While I strongly believed in the product I was selling, I won deals because I developed trust with my clients. I treated sales like a true human, energetic exchange, and built genuine relationships as a result.

I was finally learning to integrate my worlds. In one space, I showed up as a badass business babe. In another, a student of self-growth and healing. I trusted my exploration into open-heart connecting and authentic relating was helping me to sell more effectively and lead creatively at work. Similarly, I was confident that my intentional conversation skills, obsession to detail, and entrepreneurial mind brought value to my community.

See, we've traditionally operated in binary realities, seeing each world —whether traditional business or creator-based economics—as fully separate from the other. Even further, we've been taught to align our identities to one side of the aisle. Since I've always rejected the idea that there is one version of any truth, I learned to create my own world by defying odds and integrating both sides.

Still though, while I had figured out how to skillfully chart my own territory, I felt I was missing a connection to my dharmic path. So in early 2020, I decided to trade in my lavish paycheck for the gift of time and took nearly ten months off—a decision that caused mom's heart to skip a beat. I bought a travel trailer and read books next to the ocean, wrote poetry in the desert, danced in the forest, and sang under the stars. I got to know myself and feel what it meant to be alive.

At the same time, the politics and turmoil of our country were at an all-time high with the rise of racial tension during the George Floyd protests where I became a loud and active participant. Driven by my deep passion for equality, my time off went from prophetic heart-based exploration to deep societal and anthropological research. My subject: the American Dream.

I deconstructed its history, tracing its origins back to the term itself. For months, my living room was filled with post-its as I read scholarly articles, political speeches, policies, poems, and watched documentaries. The meaning was controversial—some sides defending dreams, others expressing nightmares. By the end, I came to a sad truth - a hopeful tribute that had become the song of our country's promise was never really about dreaming at all. It was a term describing a system of economics that gave access to some at the expense of others. By selling generations of people on a version of reality that was only attainable to a select few, it perpetuated the division, inequity, and inequality that made the dream possible. It favored stability over innovation and obedience over creativity. Thus, the solution became vividly clear—we must create a new version of the collective, a new American Dream.

At first, I couldn't understand how to approach something so massive. Like any issue plaguing our generation, it felt daunting and overwhelming. I thought back to my time in sales. I remembered the courage it took to build my path in an antiquated field. On the one hand, it felt trivial and disconnected. On the other, I realized that it included a potent lesson about our collective path forward. See for me, sales was never really about mastering persuasion or control—though much of its background, or at least reputation, is based on these principles. Instead, my time in sales was an experiment in human connection. Multiple times a day, I get on the phone with varying titles at various size companies, all with unique problems and goals. While I undoubtedly had an agenda of selling software, I learned how to use these conversations as a microcosm of the human experience.

Rather than drive my interests, I sought to deeply understand theirs. I did deep research ahead of the call to understand their background. I asked questions about who they were, and what mattered to them - with no agenda other than genuine curiosity. I learned why they took the call and what problems they were looking to solve. Sometimes we weren't always aligned, and as soon that became clear, I honestly shared. When it made sense to continue, I transitioned from selling to this person to selling with as we collaboratively won internal budgets and approvals. In the process, I created long-lasting relationships built on genuine trust.

Through this lens, I started to wonder—together, could we collectively learn to rewire connections the same way? Could we learn to put aside our interests, whether social, political, financial, or otherwise, and deeply understand the motivations of the other? And if we could learn to integrate our interests as multi-faceted, creative, and compassionate beings, couldn't we rebuild the systems and structures that have shaped our foundations for centuries? Could heart-forward leadership be the most courageous way to create a new American Dream, a reality that was accessible to all?

Now listen, in no way am I proposing that the key to generations of inequity and misappropriation are solved simply by tuning into our hearts. There is real, deep work that is required by each of us to own our parts of history. We must all be deeply devoted to creating more inclusive and accessible worlds for all. What I am suggesting, however, is that we use our shared humanness as a start. Our compass then is the heart.

The reality is, there is no time to avoid this conversation. We must learn to be greater than any one version of the truth, way of living, or being. It is time for a different kind of solution—a new version of leadership. Above all, there is only one thing that we all share: being human. Now more than ever, we must be willing to enter into our unique lines of work with this singular focus—unified by our humanness. When we're aligned from this place, we create the strongest and most meaningful change because when you influence the heart, you move the individual. When you move the individual, you motivate the collective.

For you, that may be ditching the 9-5 culture entirely and building your dream business, or dedicating your life's mission to social justice. For others, it may be bringing consciously aligned practices to board rooms. No matter where you show up, may you have the courage and bravery to do it differently. For each time you do, you become a flutter of disruption in our collective consciousness. Your pink blazer and dialed sales presentation threw off the executive who rolled their eyes at your boldness. Your provocative post causes the conservative-minded follower to question their relationship with themselves. Every time you choose expression over suppression, you showcase your unique version of humanness and create safety for others to do the same. It is this safety of being our version of being human that is where our true work starts.

Of course, we all must recognize that this work is bigger than racy posts and playful outfits in traditional settings. It's about learning to clean up our energy individually, so we can interact with others without agenda. Whether selling a product or service or reshaping collective belief systems, we all share a deep desire to be seen and understood. When we show up with expectations for the other person (that they buy, or who they 'be' in the world), we are not showing up from a place of aligned service. Instead, we are projecting a desired outcome onto the other person leaving them to feel unheard or unseen in who they are and what they are seeking.

If instead, we truly believe that the best interest of someone else is also the interest of ourselves, then we can embrace someone's yes or no with equal acceptance. We no longer seek their buy-in for our validation. We stand firm in our offering, solid in our truth, and loving in our energy. From this place, we can curiously inquire into the hearts and minds of the other. Without needing to fully agree or align to understand, we create a mutually safe place for both interests to be fully expressed. Through this space, we build a deeper presence through transparency and a true path to intimacy.

When this is your focus, the intention of the conversation fundamentally shifts. It becomes focused on the true heart of the matter, regardless of the outcome. One connection, one expression, and one heart-based leader at a time, we create a new version of the American Dream—one that is accessible, inclusive, and available to all.

This is our conscious social responsibility. We are the brave activists, fearless artists, and heart-centered leaders here to create a new reality. Through our becoming, we can build a reality that unifies us through our differences, equalizes our inequities, and connects us all on a truly human level.

So whether you lead teams, grow flowers, or join the circus, I hope you choose heart-based leadership.

* * *

I TRAVELED to the water

Through fields and mountain tops

To sit down with my Soul

And have a heart to heart

I HAD to rid distractions

Removing busy work

I stood face to face with restless

To let my wisdom have a word

AT FIRST MY ego started talking

Distracting me as truth

So I waited for the feeling

Of my aching wound

EVENTUALLY IT CAME

The way clouds always do

Tempting me to mask it

Running from my inner truth

THIS TIME I chose to listen

This time I chose to stay

Stripped of all my stories

Cracked open and displayed

I LOOKED into my scars

With compassion in my eyes

For they light up my path of darkness

Just like the stars in black night skies

I ASKED into what I wanted

If my Soul could have her way

My deepest ask I did not know

Waiting as she gathered what to say

"YOU'VE LET GO of all your wild

You've stopped listening

Lost in all your stories

Of deep abandoning

WE KNOW that you adapted

In the way that you knew how

But the war is finally over

The time to start living is right now

YOU GET to have the magic

HEART-CENTERED LEADERSHIP

And experience your dreams

You get to be supported

As unlikely as its seems

So what would it be like

To start living from this place

Believing in a type of love

Built on forgiveness and grace

Your place in this world is sacred

Your living purposeful

The superpowers of your heart

Are palpably transformable

Your mission is to capture

The beauty in and of this world

Leaving every interaction

With the grace of your Soul's word

So carry on dear one

By listening to the deepest pain

Our guidance comes in many forms

Like learning to dance in the rain"

. . .

Eventually she departed

Her weathering passed too

Bringing movement to my energy

The way clouds always do

I smiled in deep reverence

Of her tender, gentle hug

Mirroring my beauty

Showing me the way back home to love

So this is why I travel to the water

Through fields and mountain tops

To practice conversation

With deepest matters of my heart

And one day I trust deeply

That I will share this epic love

And for now my heart continues pointing

Toward the North Star above

MARA ELAINE WILLEMIN

Mara Elaine Willemin is the founder and creative director of Mara Elaine Media, advisor for creative entrepreneurs, and revenue leader for early-stage start-ups. She helps conscious founders & CEOs develop purpose-driven, go-to-market motions to scale their brands through story-led sales. By using the power of words, the art of cinematography, and the heart of purpose-driven storytelling, Mara believes in creating a new culture of growth. She has scaled start-ups from early-stage through successful acquisitions, spoken on conferences stages, and been featured on podcasts such as The Product-Led Revenue Show and Soul Purpose Driven. Mara lives in Denver, Colorado with her partner Frankie and two dogs, Josie and Moose.

Website: www.maraelaine.com

Instagram: @magicwithmara

ABOUT EXALTED PUBLISHING HOUSE

*E*xalted Publishing House produces books that move hearts and minds. We are a *hybrid* book publisher for leaders, CEOS, entrepreneurs and business owners who want to get more eyes on their story. We offer support with solo books as well as collaborative books like Heart-Centered Leadership.

Exalted Publishing House has a simple philosophy: change the world through words. Our aim is to work with a small number of entrepreneurs, organizations and businesses each year to uphold the highest standard of intimacy and personalization in the cathartic writing and publishing process. We mainly work in the realms of the alternative, disenfranchised & different by sharing stories that aren't always spoken through mainstream channels.

What sets us apart:

We focus on supporting our clients with messaging, storytelling and visibility/publicity. We believe books are a tool to bring more awareness to a brand. We help support than brand become media ready, standout and be a go-to business in their industry.

Connect:

Website: Exalted Publishing House

Instagram: @exaltedpublishinghouse

ABOUT KATELYN ANNEMARIE BRUSH

Behind every book lies a visionary.

Katelyn AnneMarie Brush was the brains and heart behind this book coming to life.

Katelyn is a visionary entrepreneur, bestselling author, and the host of the podcast, *Soul Purpose Driven*. Her Leadership and Business Coaching programs have helped hundreds of leaders align with their values, goals, and desired life. Recently, she launched an agency, Nurtured Marketing, which brings digital marketing services to companies both big and small across industries (real estate, therapy, coaching and more) so they can create engaged and excited audiences. Her expertise lies in helping business owners expand their reach, while making more impact and income doing what they were put on the planet to do. One of her favorite achievements has been building an incredible community of like-minded people who want to make a positive change in the world and she is proud to have brought many of them together to write this book. Born and raised in New York, she now lives a peaceful mountain town life in Colorado with her cat son, Loki.

Website: www.katelynannemarie.com

Nurtured Agency: www.katelynannemarie.com/nurtured-marketing

Podcast: www.podcasts.apple.com/us/podcast/soul-purpose-driven/id1522519739

Made in the USA
Middletown, DE
18 November 2022

15494770R00149